MEMORIES OF
SUNDERLAND

TRUE NORTH BOOKS

DEAN CLOUGH
HALIFAX
WEST YORKSHIRE
HX3 5AX
TEL 01422 344344

The Publishers would like to thank the following companies for supporting the production of this book

Argyle House School

Arnott Insurance

Blacklock Jewellers

City of Sunderland College

Corning Limited

Cottam Brothers Limited

Coutts & Findlater Limited

Duckworths Funeral Directors

WH Forster (Printers) Limited

JG Haswell

Northumbrian Water Limited

Sunderland Marine Mutual Insurance

AE Taylor & Company (Sunderland) Limited

Edward Thompson Group Limited

Thursby's Furnishings

University of Sunderland

Vaux Breweries Limited

Fred Williamson & Sons Limited

First published in Great Britain by True North Books
Dean Clough
Halifax HX3 5AX
1998

ISBN 1 900 463 71 7

Introduction

Welcome to *Memories of Sunderland,* a look back on some of the places, events and people in the city which have shaped our lives over a period of around half a century. The following pages are brought to life by a selection of images from the not-too-distant past, chosen according to their ability to rekindle fond memories of days gone by and show how people used to shop, work and play in the area where they grew up.

Coronation celebrations on Bridge Street in May 1953

Modern image reproduction techniques have enabled us to present these pictures in a way rarely seen before, and the lively design and informative text has attempted to set the book apart from some of the other works available.

The chosen period is one which generally contains events within the memory of a large number of people in Sunderland - this is not a book about crinolines or bowler-hats! Neither is *Memories of Sunderland* a work of local history in the normal sense of the term. It has far more to do with entertainment than serious study, but we hope you will agree it is none the worse for that.

It is hoped that the following pages will prompt readers own memories of Sunderland from days gone by - and we are always delighted to hear from people who can add to the information contained in the captions so that we can enhance future editions of the book.

Many local companies and organisations have allowed us to study their archives and include their history - and fascinating reading it makes too. The present-day guardians of the firms concerned are proud of their products, the achievements of their people and the hard work of their forefathers whose efforts created these long established organisations in the first place. We are pleased to play our part by making it possible for them to share their history with a wider audience.

When we began compiling *Memories of Sunderland* several months ago we anticipated that the task would be a pleasurable one, but our expectations were greatly surpassed. There is a growing appetite for all things 'nostalgic' and we are pleased to have played a small part in swelling the number of images and associated information available to the growing number of enthusiasts.

There is much talk in modern times about the regeneration of the local economy, the influx of new industries and the challenge of attracting new enterprise from other regions to Sunderland. And quite right too. We could, however, make the mistake of thinking that the changes are all happening *now,* but the reality is that there have always been major developments going on in the city. 'Change' is relentless and the photographs on the pages in the book serve to remind us of some of them.

Memories of Sunderland has been a pleasure to compile, we sincerely hope you enjoy reading it.

Happy memories!

COVER DESIGN/PHOTOGRAPHS COMPILED BY MARK SMITH
CAPTIONS COMPILED BY PHIL HOLLAND AND PAULINE BELL
TEXT PAGES DESIGNED BY MANDY WALKER AND NICKY BRIGHTON
LOCAL BUSINESS CONTENT ORGANISED BY GARETH MARTIN

Contents

The remains of the Blue Bell Hotel, Roker Avenue, after the devastation caused by a German bombing raid on the night of 7th November 1941. The exposed beams in the roof of the substantial property and the collapsed floors beneath it give a vivid impression of just how powerful the explosion had been, and the precariously-poised dresser on the second floor shows what a lucky escape the staff had had just a few hours earlier.

Around the city centre

Christ Church as it appeared on a very wet day in June 1964. The small old-fashioned saloon car in the picture could have misled us into thinking that the photograph was much older than this, though the light-coloured Vauxhall Cresta in the distance is a certain giveaway as to the correct era. The dramatic spire of Christ Church has dominated the area from its Stockton Road location since it was built in the mid 1860s. When it opened, Christ Church served the growing population which surrounded it in the increasingly fashionable Ashbrooke area and was one of only a handful of churches noted for their beauty at the time.

An enchanting scene along Holmeside dating from around half a century ago. Several familiar businesses can be seen in the view and nostalgic 'street furniture' such as the old style traffic lights, street lamps and tramlines add to the feelings of nostalgia evoked by the picture. The busy corner site, known as Waterloo Place on the right of the picture was occupied by Maynards the toffee makers. Above Maynards' sunblind the Hornby Train sign belonging to Saxons, who also boasted a 'home cinema department' at this location. Notice the police cyclist on the right of the picture approaching the traffic lights and the variety of period motor cars which give the scene real character.

Below: This 1950s view shows the Wheatsheaf junction and a fine double decker tramcar moving past the town's transport offices. The heavily-shaded confectionery shop on the right of the picture stands beside a *tram stop* - those words looking rather odd to modern eyes.

Note the lighthouse corner building on the extreme left of the picture. This was always a busy road junction, taking traffic straight on towards South Shields and Tyneside beyond, with local Roker traffic heading off to the right.

SHOP AT BINNS
SEABURN FULWELL

TRAM STOP

R R Clark/Beamish Museum

> **"THE GRAND HOTEL WAS A WELL-KNOWN LANDMARK IN SUNDERLAND FOR MANY YEARS UNTIL ITS CLOSURE IN 1969"**

Above: A rare picture of the Grand Hotel, seen in the background of this 1950s photograph which also features Tramcar No. 92, on the Seaburn and Fulwell route. With 50 bedrooms and a busy public bar the establishment was popular with local people and visitors alike. *The Grand* was demolished soon after it closed its doors for the last time in 1969. The imposing facade was a well-known landmark in Sunderland and the building was one of many on Bridge Street which had to be cleared in order to make room for the new inner ring road.

Beamish Museum

Left: This picture dates from about 1950 and features the Lambton Arms on Crowtree Road. The Truman's House stood next to the King's Theatre which was damaged beyond repair in a wartime bombing raid in May 1943. The theatre stood derelict for a further decade before being pulled down in 1954, followed by the Lambton Arms itself less than two decades later.

Above: This busy scene was recorded around 1930 and shows East and West High Street with Mackie's Corner on the right. A variety of architectural styles combine to give the picture added interest, including the domed Hutchinson building on the left with the clock indicating 3.26p.m. Most of the buildings appear to be stained black from the smoke and grime created by hundreds of chimneys in the area over many decades. Several of the businesses featured in the scene may be remembered by modern readers. Manfield and Son's the clothiers can be seen on the left, with Goodson's *for style and value* across the street. Nearest the position of the camera, on the right, a sale was being held at F. Walker and Co. - the 'juvenile clothier.'

Beamish Museum

Above left: A charming scene from the 1940s which shows people going about their day to day activities along High Street West. The short shadows and extended sun blinds suggest that this was a warm summer's day. Typical of the time is the fact that most of the passers-by are wearing hats or caps. It was considered rather unusual for people to go about bare-headed in those days. Evidence of the Tramway Era is featured with the smooth curved rails and overhead power cables clearly in view. The first services to be operated by the newly-created Sunderland Tramways Company began in April 1879, running on the Roker, Christ Church, Tatham Street and Docks routes. Initially horse-drawn trams were used, but, by 1900 electrically driven tramcars began to be introduced.

Left: A lone tram showing a *Roker* destination board is featured in this picture. The scene is dominated by the tangle of overhead wires and cables necessary to take the electric current to the tramcars, and the sea of slippery cobblestones which made for a bumpy ride in the motorcars of the day. A sign on the pole on the left of the picture advises drivers to drive slowly and it often surprises people to learn that there were many more road fatalities in the 1940s and 1950s than there are today, despite there being less than half the number of vehicles on the roads at the time.

Above: "Danger Men At Work" was the message when this picture was taken sometime towards the end of the 1940s. It is immediately obvious just how much the method of 'roadworks' has changed in the course of five or six decades. Apart from the rather dismal sign there are no bright warnings to oncoming traffic of the hazard they have to negotiate. The only concession to added visibility is the pair of white gloves worn by the point-duty policeman in the centre of the picture!

Below: This relatively modest entrance belonged to Black's Regal Cinema. With seats for 2,500 this was the largest and most elegant of the cinemas in Sunderland. It was the talk of the town when it opened in 1932, having taken around 12 months to construct at the considerable cost of over £100,000. The first film to be shown here was 'One Good Turn' starring Laurel and Hardy. In common with most establishments of this kind the Regal contained a large Compton Organ which would rise up out of the floor at the beginning of the programme. In 1959 the Rank organisation took over the cinema and the name changed to Odeon. The cinema continued to operate in much the same way until February 1975 when it closed for conversion to three screen operation, re-opening as such just a month later. Sadly this was not enough to attract enough customers to keep the cinema going, and the cinema closed in 1982.

Beamish Museum

> **"WITH SEATS FOR 2,500 *THE REGAL CINEMA* WAS THE LARGEST AND MOST ELEGANT OF SUNDERLAND'S PICTURE HOUSES"**

Above: Typical of 1930s cinema architecture, the Ritz was one of Sunderland's better appointed establishments available to the film-going public. The cinema opened at this corner of Holmeside in 1937 and the photograph was taken in March of that year. With a seating capacity of 1700 the Ritz fell into the medium sized category of cinemas in the heyday of new openings that existed at this time. As with most other surviving cinemas several name changes and various changes of ownership have taken place here, and readers may know it as the 'ABC' or the 'Cannon.'

No book on the Sunderland area would be complete without a picture of the Sunderland Empire, and this one shows the theatre as it appeared with a rather more grimy appearance in November 1964. The Empire was opened in July 1907, billed, imaginatively as The Place To Spend A Pleasant Evening. Vesta Tilley - "London's idol and ideal male impersonator" - topped the opening-night bill. Only ten months earlier she had laid the foundation stone for what would become one of the country's best known places of entertainment.

Above: Warm sunshine was the order of the day when this picture was taken in the summer of 1965. The location of the scene is unmistakably Fawcett Street. The full length of the Binns store needed the protection of these thick canvas sunshades as the temperature reached its peak in this mid-day view from around 35 years ago. Several buses can be seen in the photograph, at least one of them carrying the very familiar slogan 'Shop at Binns' which had been a feature of local transport advertising messages for longer than most people could remember. Just overtaking the single deck bus in the foreground is an Austin 1100 saloon, a common sight on Britain's roads at this time and streets ahead of other saloons made by rival manufacturers in terms of ride, spaciousness and economy. Keen eyes may be able to make out the gently-curving outline of the Wearmouth Bridge in the far distance. The bridge was opened in 1929 by the Duke of York, later to become King George VI.

Oops. The 1967 E-type Jaguar came off much worse than the older and less valuable Ford Prefect which appears to have attempted to drive up its bonnet. The sleek Jaguar, capable of speeds of up to 150m.p.h has often been described as the world's most beautiful sports car. The accident occurred in the Bridge Street/St. Mary's way area in the late 1960s and caused predictable, but unwelcome interest from passing pedestrians in the area.

Above: In a photograph taken in May 1966 the stark and very functional outline of properties on the Gilley Law housing estate are featured as they approach completion. The picture is interesting for a number of reasons, not least of which being the fact that this represented what amounted to the final burst of new house building activity by the Council in the post-war period. The Council had decided to spend a record £6.2 million on housing during the two years preceding this picture, on work which included 890 flats at Gilley Law. Other developments which were in the process of construction at this time included those at Witherwack, Mill Hill, Downhill and Town End Farm. Sunderland had been embarked upon a major slum clearance programme since the early 1950s and part and parcel of that essential work was to create large numbers of homes for the displaced residents. The magnitude of the challenge should not be underestimated, and those quick to criticise the style and layout of the homes featured here should try to visualise some of the overcrowded, damp, insanitary and often infested 'homes' they replaced.

> **"SUNDERLAND COUNCIL EMBARKED ON A MAJOR SLUM CLEARANCE IN THE EARLY 1950s"**

Below: Work was nearing completion on the exterior signs of the Trustee Savings Bank when this photograph was taken in 1965. At the halfway point of the 1960s there was good reason to be positive about the prospects for the town as she, like the rest of Britain started to 'swing.' Highlights included the creation of 500 jobs at the British and International Addressing Company at Hendon Road, 100 additional jobs came to town with the arrival of the Olin Mathieson Mine Equipment Company and Ericcson's Telephone Equipment of North Hylton Road announced plans to employ an extra 800 staff. During the year the keys to the 20,000th Sunderland council house were handed over and the order books at local ship yards were described as being healthier than they had been for a decade.

A familiar view of Fawcett Street, with one of Sunderland's best known landmarks at the time, the Town Hall building and it's distinctive clock tower. The Town Hall and municipal buildings were opened on November 6th 1890. The construction work had taken three years and cost £30,000. Within a decade of the opening the building was found to be too small for the growing number of functions carried on by the local authority, and departments had to be housed at other locations. At the turn of the century consideration was given to the possibility of extending the original building but this never came to fruition. The end of the 1960s saw intense and passionate debate about the future of the old Town Hall building and many people were amazed at the suggestion that it may be pulled down. Those who were became dismayed when the decision was taken to pull it down, and it finally disappeared amid tremendous controversy, in 1971.

Above: An expanse of cobbles as far as the eye can see, combined with the delightful old advertisements and the tramlines in the picture give this view a very appealing appearance. The photograph was taken on the stretch of road opposite Rowlandson Terrace. Some of the advertisements on the hoardings make interesting reading. Few people will remember the *Evening World* newspaper, the message on their advert reads "Your wife, yourself, your family are all protected by the Evening World. First and best evening paper for free insurance."

These free insurance offers were fairly common among newspapers of around half a century ago. The insurance usually related to accidental deaths and so claims were relatively rare. Another promotional idea featured on these advertisements was described on the board next to *Evening World* sign. It related to the well-known jewellery chain H. Samuels who were offering 'lucky wedding rings' with free gifts with each one from their premises at 2 Havelock Buildings.

"THE FAIRWORLD COMPANY TOOK OVER THE STUDIO CINEMA IN 1977"

Right: This picture dates from 13 January 1969 - the day of the opening of the 'Studio 1' and 'Studio 2' cinema. The establishment was owned and operated by the Star organisation and was located in the former Sans Street Mission at the bottom of High Street. The first features to be shown here were *The Impossible Years* with David Niven and *A Man and A Woman*. In later years adult movies were shown here when the name of the cinema was changed to Studio X. The Fairworld company took over the running of the cinema in 1977 and after around four years a further change took place when the Eros Cinema club took over and continued to show adult films.

Below: The dignified lines of the old Town Hall on Fawcett Street are displayed to their best effect by this photograph. It was taken in July 1971 and features several motor vehicles from the time which add to the atmosphere of the scene. This was one of hundreds of pictures taken of the Town Hall in 1971 when the threat, and then the confirmation of its forthcoming demolition became widely known. The controversy surrounding the decision to pull the building down was unsurpassed by any other event in the town's history. The Council met at the Civic Centre built on a large site opposite Mowbray Park from this time onwards. Note the sign on the building, just left of centre which reads 'sold for development by Hillier and Partner', and the advertising board on the right of the picture designed to promote the Sunderland Building Society.

By the riverside

Above: The Wearmouth Bridge from an unusual angle is featured in this picture from the late 1930s. At the time that this picture was taken the bridge had only been open for about a decade. In order to maintain the flow of traffic over this busy river crossing the engineers had constructed the new bridge over the less elegant box-section design of the old bridge. 1929 saw the dismantling of the old bridge and the opening of the new one in a ceremony performed by the Duke of York. Some impression of the vast number of rivets used in the construction of the bridge is apparent in this picture. The final rivet to be hammered home was made from silver and used to add interest to the already grand opening ceremony. A special platform had to be built to allow access to this final element of the new bridge.

Left: Construction of the Wearmouth Bridge was approaching the final stages when this picture was taken in November 1928. The structure was designed by Mott, Hay and Anderson and opened in 1929 by the Duke of York. With a touch of north east genius it had been decided to construct the new bridge around the old one, so that the flow of traffic would not be interrupted during the works. This is an interesting scene for reasons other than the inclusion of the bridge. Most of the figures in the photograph are unaware of the presence of the photographer and this image of brief moment in time has a very natural appearance as a consequence. You have to give credit to the management of *Binns* for having the idea of putting their name on everything that moved in the area. Their publicity material crops up time and again in pictures of Sunderland and this must have kept them one step ahead of the competition in the 'awareness' stakes for many years. The building on the left of the picture, looking out across the slippery damp cobbles was the Bridge End Vaults public house. The popular watering hole was pulled down in 1967 to make way for part of the new inner ring road scheme.

Above: The wide expanse of water and three ships at various stages of their construction will rekindle memories of days gone by among workers who once toiled in this industrial heart of Sunderland. This view was recorded in 1964. The number of shipyards operating in the area had been in decline since the end of the Second World War. A ray of hope was seen in 1964 when an order for bulk carriers worth £4 million was secured by the Southwick Yard of Austin and Pickersgill. Amalgamations and closures were responsible for the reduction in yards and the staff who worked in them. Nationalisation arrived in 1977 and Sunderland's remaining shipyards became known as *British Shipbuilders,* before making another change of name to North East Shipbuilders Ltd. The future of the organisation looked assured when an order to supply a Danish firm with 24 ferries was secured. Complications arose and the order was only partially completed. The last of the vessels was delivered in 1990 and this proved to be one of the final acts of the once great shipbuilding industry in the area.

Beamish Museum

> ## "ASSOCIATED INDUSTRIES SUCH AS ROPE MAKING AND SAILMAKING GREW UP ALONGSIDE THE SHIPYARDS"

Above: A rare photograph of considerable local historic value. It shows the construction work taking place on the Wearmouth Bridge in 1928 as the major undertaking approaches completion. The picture is taken from an unusual angle and shows much of the workmens' clutter and scaffolding in place as they complete the job. The absence of people or activity in the scene suggests that it may have been taken on a Sunday, but this is pure speculation. The photograph gives a clear view of the original box-section bridge which remained in place until the new structure was completed. The rail bridge on the left of the picture is referred to less frequently than its big sister on the right. The rail bridge is much older of course, having been constructed in 1879.

A hive of activity along the banks of the river is shown in this atmospheric scene. The view is dominated by the large ship moored in the distance and the sturdy cranes shown perched along the quay side. By the time this picture was taken the shipbuilding industry in Sunderland had existed for around 150 years, surviving many fluctuations in its fortunes as the demand for vessels rose and fell. In the earliest years of the industry the ships were constructed using timber and traditional techniques. Associated industries developed and grew at the same time as the shipyards, such as rope making, sail making and the fabrication of all types of ironmongery and fittings.

Below: A stirring sight indeed, to anyone with a passion for Sunderland's shipbuilding past and a feeling for the influence that the river and the sea has had on the character of the area. The picture was taken from the Alexandra Bridge and shows in some detail the hull of a large vessel as it nears completion.

In the distance two medium-sized vessels, one registered in Newcastle (and of uncertain name) nearest the quayside, and the other *The Jersey Spray* registered in London. Sunderland's shipbuilding industry has had a chequered history and the ups and downs of its prosperity has had a knock-on effect on the economy of the area. Wartime rejuvenated the fortunes of the nine remaining yards in Sunderland and their increased order books carried on through to the mid 1950s.

From the 1960s onwards the future of the industry looked uncertain, and by the 1970s the outlook was decidedly precarious. All major shipbuilding activity ceased during the following decade, much to the sadness of thousands of families and individuals who had been associated with the industry for as long as they could remember.

Events and occasions

Tony Wickens/Beamish Museum

Above: Genuine expressions of joy can be seen in the faces of the youngsters in this picture as they greeted King George VI and Queen Elizabeth. The boys were residents at Sunderland Boys Orphanage and they are seen here providing the Guard of Honour for the royal visitors. The visit took place on February 22nd 1939 at the training centre on Gray Road. The Naval uniforms worn by the boys were to have a special significance as the clouds of war gathered over Europe. Within seven months war would be declared between Britain and Germany and the lives of all those pictured here would be thrown into turmoil.

> **"KING GEORGE VI AND QUEEN ELIZABETH VISITED SUNDERLAND IN FEBRUARY 1939"**

Beamish Museum

Above: The crowds were out in force when this picture was taken on the sea front at Roker. The photograph is thought to date from the 1930s. It gives a good view of Roker Pier and the distinctive lighthouse which has guarded this stretch of coastline since it was constructed in 1903. Simple pleasures have been enjoyed by Sunderland people at this location for generations. Boating trips in the sea have always been popular, as were long walks in the bracing fresh air or ball games in the nearby park. Many readers will remember paddling in the shallow pool along the seafront promenade or picnics on the beach as weary parents enjoyed a well-earned rest in the warm sunshine. Happy days!

Below: King George VI and Queen Elizabeth (later the Queen Mother) played an important role during the years of the Second World War, touring the country and visiting areas which had suffered great losses during enemy bombing raids. They are seen here receiving a typically rousing welcome from shipyard workers when they visited Sunderland in April 1943. Shortly before this scene was recorded the royal couple watched a parade of Civil Defence workers in John Street and were taken on a guided tour of badly damaged parts of the district so that they could see the effects of the Nazi onslaught for themselves.

Both pictures: "Tell your hubby we are delivering the goods." This was the message from the shipbuilders of Sunderland to the wife of the Prime Minister, Clementina Churchill when she visited the area in April 1941. The visit was one of many undertaken by Mrs Churchill to industrial areas in Britain as part of her morale-boosting campaign. The shipyards of Sunderland were rejuvenated during the Second World War by a tremendous volume of orders. Most of the extra work involved the construction of merchant ships - around 250 vessels were built during the war period, more than a quarter of the total output of the British shipbuilding industry during the war years. The number of active shipyards more than doubled from 4 to 9 during the course of the war, bringing with it employment for women as well as men in the process. New techniques were employed in order to speed-up the production of ships which were needed to replace those lost at sea. Welding became much more common in the yards because the technique was far quicker than the traditional rivetting method, and every effort was made to break new records in the time taken to produce each vessel. The first half of 1941 was one of the worst periods of the war for most people in Sunderland. The town was subjected to one of the heaviest and mostly prolonged bombing campaigns by the enemy which saw many deaths and widespread damage to residential and commercial property in the district.

Below: The launch of a ship is always a very special occasion, no matter how many times one has attended such an event. This photograph is over half a century old, it was taken at the launch of the S.S Ingivi in July 1947. The vessel was built at the yard of John Crown and Sons in Sunderland and the owner was Rolf Wigand of Bergen. Officials from the yard and a party from the ship owners in Norway can be seen at the launching ceremony. Shipbuilding began on a significant scale in Sunderland during the late 1700s. At the turn of the next century the output of local yards was just under 15,000 tons from 24 ship yards employing around 650 people. Sunderland's importance as a port was growing rapidly thorough these years and by 1830 it was ranked as fourth busiest in the country.

> "AT THE TURN OF THE 19TH CENTURY, SUNDERLAND HAD 24 SHIP YARDS EMPLOYING JUST 650 PEOPLE"

Above: Efforts to rebuild Britain's commercial and industrial strength after the end of the Second World War were supported by a series of trade fairs and exhibitions. At this time Sunderland's economy was dominated by the shipbuilding industry with around 1 in 5 male workers being involved in it. Every local authority was encouraged, if not obliged, to organise a presence at these events capable of reflecting the skill and craftsmanship of the people and workers in their particular town or city. This exhibition stand was organised by the North East Development Board in the late 1940s or early 1950s. In the distance we can detect the nationwide composition of the event from the presence of a trade stand promoting the industrial attractions of Coventry. In the foreground a display of ropes and ropemaking tools can be seen. It was natural that, with Sunderland's seafaring activities and importance as a port, that the ropemaking industry would develop in the area - and so it did.

A beautifully decorated flat in Wear Garth, Sunderland in June 1953. The occasion was the Coronation of Queen Elizabeth and the residents of the street were taking part in a 'Best Decorated House' competition. The competition was run by Sunderland Corporation as part of the Coronation programme and streets and houses around the district were similarly adorned. This was a time of great pride for the country and everyone was caught up in Coronation fever. It is a sobering thought to imagine that the tiniest member of this happy group would now be around fifty years old.

Left: Portraits of the 'new' Queen Elizabeth adorn the lamp standards along Bridge Street in 1953. This charming picture of the centre of Sunderland captures some of the atmosphere from the time, with the 'Roker' tram and 1940s motorcar adding a degree of character to the scene which manages to bring the whole thing to life for us. The Central Hotel can be seen on the other side of the street. It was one of the few such establishments to survive the demolition craze which saw the demise of the Three Crowns, The Bridge End Vaults, The Bells and several other popular watering holes.

Above: This delightful photograph is certain to rekindle memories of the 1950s in general, and of the local celebrations which marked the coronation of Her Majesty Queen Elizabeth II in 1953 in particular. This picture was taken on May 26th 1953 on Bridge Street. On entering the town over the river bridge it seemed as if the whole of Sunderland was festooned in red, white and blue as the local population joyfully entered the spirit of the royal celebrations. The Grand Hotel was no exception - it is shown on the left of the picture complete with garlands and bunting. Nearer to the camera, the Bridge End Vaults, with its distinctive cream-tiled walls is visible, and a young girl poses with her brother and pet dog for the picture.

> **"ON ENTERING THE TOWN OVER THE RIVER IT SEEMED AS IF THE WHOLE OF SUNDERLAND WAS FESTOONED IN RED, WHITE AND BLUE"**

Above: "Unity is Strength" proclaimed the banner being carried by members of Sunderland Trades Council on this protest march in February 1968. The marchers were protesting at the increasing levels of unemployment in the town at the time. Newspaper reports from the time described the disappointment felt by the organisers as only 39 people had turned out for the protest, despite the previous months' jobless total passing the 6,300 mark. Up until the establishment of the Sunderland's well-documented new industries - such as car manufacturing - her achilles heel was always her reliance on traditional heavy industries such as shipbuilding and coal mining. These were subject to fluctuations in their fortunes which were beyond the control of the people employed there. What made matters worse was the fact that, often, several members of the same family would be employed in these industries and whole communities would suffer when the industries encountered difficulties. Five years before this picture was taken unemployment stood at around 9000 people in Sunderland, but five years later, in the early 1970s, this would more than double. Few of the concerned marchers here would have believed it possible that motorcar production would become a central part Sunderland's recovery within two decades of this demonstration taking place.

Right: With flags flying and miles of bunting and floral garlands on display, the people of Sunderland threw themselves into the coronation celebrations in the summer of 1953. This scene was captured along Bridge Street on May 27th 1953. The road and rail bridges across the Wear can be seen in the distance. The little lad in the picture looks happy to be out with his dad, and relaxed enough to twist his face for the photographer. It is a sobering thought to think that he will be well into his fifties at the time of writing, with children or even grandchildren of his own.

Wartime

Above: A rather sorry sight depicted by this picture showing the Binns Store on Borough Road after it was severely damaged by an enemy bombing raid. The photograph dates from April 1941 and the aftermath of the bombing raid is all too apparent; shattered windows at all levels and a normally busy shopping street cordoned off to protect passers-by from falling glass. There was something quite symbolic about the destruction of Sunderland's best-known department store. It was a talking point among people in the town who felt as if they shared a common loss. The damage to the store had been caused by several German incendiary bombs which caused a massive fire which quickly caught hold of the massive department store.

Left: Some impression of the sheer devastation caused to the lives and property of ordinary people can be had from this breathtaking picture. It shows the aftermath of a Second World War bomb blast and was taken in August 1940 in the Viewforth Terrace area. Sunderland's housing stock suffered dreadfully from the Nazi bombers, as did her retail and commercial properties. A staggering 34,500 houses were damaged of which around 1000, like this one, were beyond repair. The provision of air raid shelters which started from the months leading up to the outbreak of hostilities helped tremendously to limit the deaths and injuries caused by the falling bombs. At least 7,000 Anderson Shelters were supplied and erected in the district; many long hours would be spent by families sheltering from the frequent attacks. The worst raids of the war took place during May 1943. Within the space of a week there were two attacks, the first killing 70 people and seriously injuring 73 others. The second raid resulted in an even greater death toll, 83 dead and 109 seriously injured. Such was the extent of this, the last air attack on Sunderland, that 3,500 people were made homeless.

"THE BLUE BELL HOTEL WAS BOMBED IN NOVEMBER 1941, SHORTLY AFTER CLOSING TIME"

The remains of the Blue Bell Hotel, Roker Avenue, after the devastation caused by a German bombing raid on the night of 7th November 1941. The well-known watering hole had stood on this spot since the turn of the century. It had replaced an earlier public house of the same name. Fortunately for the regulars of the Blue Bell the bomb had exploded there shortly *after* closing time. The three members of staff who were on the premises at the time escaped serious injury. A small crowd has gathered in this picture to watch the workmen as they attempt to make the building safe. The exposed beams in the roof of the substantial property and the collapsed floors beneath it give a vivid impression of just how powerful the explosion had been, and the precariously-poised dresser on the second floor shows what a lucky escape the staff had had just a few hours earlier.

Shopping spree

Below: The hustle and bustle of Bridge Street is captured in this 1950s photograph. Much of the property along the right hand side of the picture was cleared in the late 1960s as efforts to ease the traffic congestion in the town centre began in earnest. The ornate facade of the Grand Hotel can be seen just left of centre. Five floors of comfortably equipped rooms, conveniently situated just a short walk away from the railway station, were well patronised from the turn of the century until the ultimate demise of the establishment in the late 1960s.

"**MUCH OF THE PROPERTY ON THE RIGHT HAND SIDE OF BRIDGE STREET WAS DEMOLISHED IN THE LATE 1960s**"

Above: The corner of Bridge Street and High Street is featured in this photograph. It dates from around 1940 and shows a variety of motor vehicles making slow progress along this busy shopping street. Tram wires are much in evidence, indeed, a double decker tramcar can just be seen heading towards the photographer in the centre of the picture. Walkers the jewellers had the busy corner site on the left of the scene and, on the right, the tallest building on Bridge Street was the Grand Hotel. For many years the *Grand* was the most respected hotel in the area, but it was demolished in 1968 with several other buildings along the west side of Bridge Street in order to make way for the new inner ring road.

An every day shopping scene dating from 1968 is featured in this delightful picture. The smart shop on this busy corner belonged to A.Healey Graham Ltd., it was located next to the equally popular Stewart Brothers fireplace shop and further along the street Levey's wallpaper stores. The 1960s fashions are apparent in the photograph; note the young lady crossing the road on the left, wearing the 'slacks' with the straps under the arches of her feet that were so popular at the time. The Vauxhall Viva at the front of the row of parked cars was the epitome of the new style of affordable saloon cars with sleek, clean lines and rectangular headlamps which characterised the late 1960s and 1970s. Sunderland's inner ring road was constructed in 1968 and this caused much disruption and upset through the town. The first section of the new road linked Bridge Street with a modern roundabout on the junction of High Street West and Gill Bridge Avenue. Much of the property along Bridge Street was pulled down, including the Bridge End Vaults, Kennedy's store and the Rose and Crown public house.

Both pictures: The distinctive wall of the Co-operative Store on the High Street is featured in these 1967 photographs. The advertising banner on the right of the above picture promotes a national 'Buy British' campaign. During the year that this picture was taken it was announced that Wearside's two biggest co-operative societies, Ryhope and Silksworth, and Sunderland were to merge. This created a massive organisation with a membership of almost 50,000 people and an annual turnover of over £3 million. Among the many benefits promised to customers and members was the prospect of reduced prices in Co-op stores and branches as a consequence of the organisation's enhanced buying power. A less-welcome milestone from this year was the closure of Monkwearmouth Station in March and the closure of Lambton Staithes in January when the volume of coal handled there fell below 2,000 tons per week. High Street retail names at the time included the Co-op, Timpsons Shoes and Marks and Spencers. In the distance of the photograph on the left British Home Stores advertising sign is just visible beyond the long queue of traffic. 1967 saw the first North Sea gas piped ashore at Easington. There followed a massive conversion programme as houses and businesses were visited by teams of fitters.

A slightly elevated view of the modern shop and residential developments in the centre of Sunderland which shows the contrast between the 'old' and the 'new' styles of property in this part of town. Blacklocks the Jewellers can be seen at the bottom left of the photograph in the late 1960s view, with Swinhoes the mens' shop across the way, beside the large branch of Halfords. The three tower blocks in the picture were part of Sunderland's post-war drive to improve the housing stock and ensure that the unsuitable and often insanitary properties of the previous century were cleared for good. Sunderland had faced more than her fair share of housing problems throughout her modern history. The outbreak of the Second World War had interrupted attempts to improve the situation and by the dawn of the 1950s there were still around a quarter of the area's houses without supplies of running water. The Council addressed the problem with an impressive degree of determination, and in the 20 year period after the end of the war had succeeded in providing 20,000 new council houses.

Bird's eye view

An aerial view of Sunderland taken from an altitude of 1200 feet. The picture dates from August 1964 and features the River Wear on the left of the scene, still with quayside cranes and river traffic on the water. The evidence of Sunderland's activities as a port and as a centre for shipbuilding abounds in the photograph. At the time this picture was taken there had been some good news for Sunderland's shipbuilders. One of the largest tankers to be launched in Britain, the 85,600 ton Borgsten was a milestone in the shipping history of Sunderland. It was constructed at a cost of £3.6 million - very modest by today's standards - for the Oslo firm of Fred Olsen. Many of the major changes which were to affect the centre of the town had not yet been initiated by the time this picture was taken, the soon-to-be-constructed inner ring road being one of the more obvious examples of this.

Above: This aerial view was taken to record the construction of the St. Mary's Way section inner ring road from, looking roughly in a southerly direction. The picture dates from about 1970. The ring road was an essential part of the drive towards speeding up the flow of traffic in the centre of Sunderland which, before the road was built, was reaching unacceptable levels. Sadly, many popular businesses and properties had to be cleared as a consequence of the road building plan, including The Grand Hotel and many other buildings along Bridge Street and Bedford Street. The Rose and Crown public house was cleared in order to make way for a roundabout. Other recognisable landmarks in this view include the 'new' Civic Centre at the top left of the picture; the original Town Hall building on Fawcett Street and the distinctive dark outline of the West Park United Reformed Church in the distance.

> **"ST. MARY'S WAY WAS BUILT IN THE EARLY 1970S TO SPEED UP THE FLOW OF TRAFFIC IN THE CITY CENTRE"**

Below: The excellent aerial view of Sunderland, looking north across the Wear was taken in about 1970. The photograph records a period of great transition in the town, the new retail heart of Sunderland was already well formed by this time with high rise tower blocks, multi-storey car parks and the new shopping centre in place. Interestingly, the new Civic Centre complex can be seen at the bottom right of the photograph, still under construction, though the much-loved original Town Hall is still present towards the top of the picture. On the left of the scene the bus station and the West Park United Reformed Church can be seen adjacent to Stockton Road. On the right of the picture is the Art Gallery and Museum, looking out across Mowbray Park.

A fascinating aerial view of Sunderland which dates from 1960. The picture affords a good view of the river and the bridges. A ship can be seen just to the right of the Wearmouth Bridge at Austin's Shipyard. Much of the property in front of the bridges, to the left and to the right of them, has been cleared. The 'new' inner ring road now gives the whole of this area a much wider and more open character than this rather crowded view of around 40 years ago. Practically in the centre of the photograph the old railway station with its distinctive roof is visible. At the bottom of the photograph, right of centre, the clock tower of the Town Hall is featured. Who could have guessed, in 1960, that the planners would later decide to pull it down.

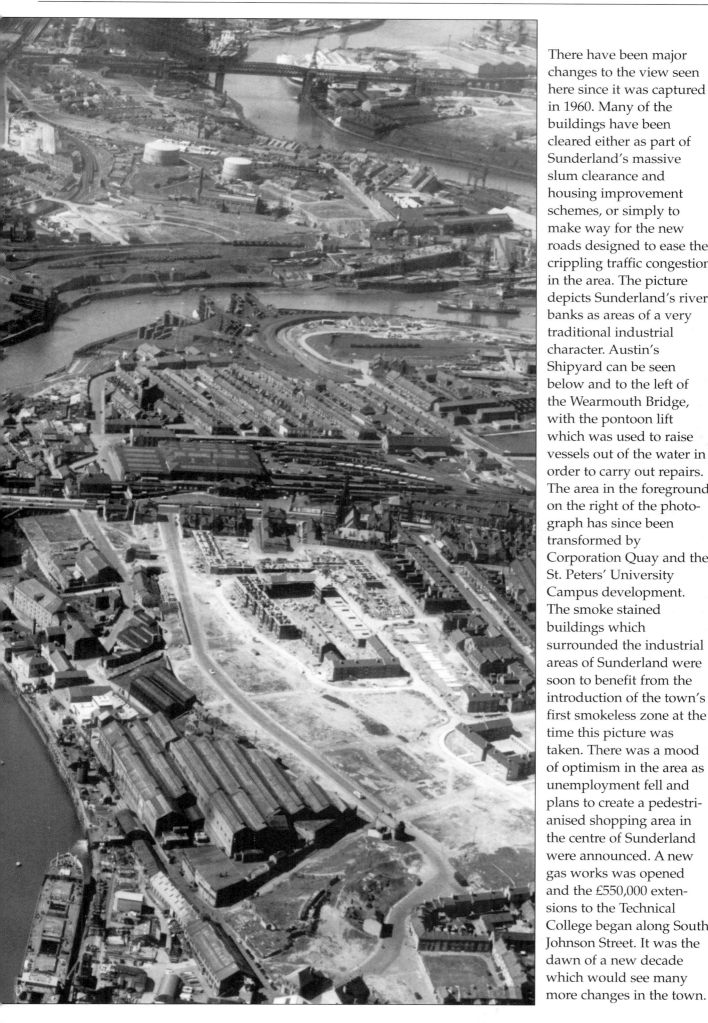

There have been major changes to the view seen here since it was captured in 1960. Many of the buildings have been cleared either as part of Sunderland's massive slum clearance and housing improvement schemes, or simply to make way for the new roads designed to ease the crippling traffic congestion in the area. The picture depicts Sunderland's river banks as areas of a very traditional industrial character. Austin's Shipyard can be seen below and to the left of the Wearmouth Bridge, with the pontoon lift which was used to raise vessels out of the water in order to carry out repairs. The area in the foreground on the right of the photograph has since been transformed by Corporation Quay and the St. Peters' University Campus development. The smoke stained buildings which surrounded the industrial areas of Sunderland were soon to benefit from the introduction of the town's first smokeless zone at the time this picture was taken. There was a mood of optimism in the area as unemployment fell and plans to create a pedestrianised shopping area in the centre of Sunderland were announced. A new gas works was opened and the £550,000 extensions to the Technical College began along South Johnson Street. It was the dawn of a new decade which would see many more changes in the town.

At work

CONTAINS
- PURE -
CANE SUGAR

WS
GRANULATED
224 LBS. NETT
WESTBURN SUGAR REF.
GREENOCK.
SCOTLAND

WS
GRANULATED
224 LBS. NETT
WESTBURN SUGAR REF. LTD.
GREENOCK.
SCOTLAND

R. FENWICK & C⁰· LTD· B

Speed 12 M.P.H.

Final touches are being made to 'Bluebottle 1' - a promotional display on the back of a 1920s flat-backed truck owned by R. Fenwick & Co. the Sunderland Brewers. The larger than life beer bottle looks quite precarious on the back of the small lorry, the solid tyres of which would have made for a bumpy ride for the 'pilot.' Still, it is unlikely that he would have been going very far or very fast, as the speed of the vehicle was restricted to a modest 12 M.P.H

A keen eye and a steady hand were required for this work. The young ladies in the scene are carefully trimming the edges and bottoms of the weighty baking bowls which surround them. These large heavy bowls would have been an important item in the cupboard of virtually every household as recently as 30 years ago, though their use has diminished in modern times as home baking has declined in popularity. Few people will appreciate the extent to which Sunderland was once involved in the ceramic industry. In the middle of the nineteenth century the manufacture of several different kinds of pottery was important to the local economy. Cheap foreign imports spelled disaster for the area's potters, most of which had gone out of business by the 1920s. The names of several of the larger local potteries may be familiar to enthusiasts for their work, examples of which are still valued by collectors; the largest of these was Scott's who survived longer than the rest, but closed around the turn of the century in the face of overwhelming competition.

Below: This five-ton forged ring had just been welded by the three men posing behind it at T.S Forster's works. Sunderland had built up a tremendous degree of expertise in many fields associated with the shipbuilding industry from the time that the first non-wooden vessels were built. The first iron ship to be built on the Wear was the Loftus, in 1852 weighing in at some 77 tons. The first steel ship was the much larger Amity, built in 1853 and weighing 479 tons. Wooden, and iron ships continued to be built, indeed, the last wooden vessel was constructed as late as 1880. The Wear's last sailing ship was built in 1893 at the Pickersgill yard.

Bottom: The 'greatest store development of modern times' proclaimed the advertisements around this construction site. Work was underway on the new Binns store when this picture was taken in 1929. The aim was 'to create two acres of additional showroom space' to accommodate the extended furnishings department. Binns was established in 1807 at modest premises in High Street, by George Binns, a draper. Larger High Street premises were acquired some 49 years later, and in 1888 the company, under the grandson of the founder, moved to an impressive property along Fawcett Street. At the turn of the century the firm employed almost 400 people and was the major name in Sunderland retailing.

An elevated view across the basement area of what had been the Binns Store, in a photograph taken in the Autumn of 1949. The picture contains a wealth of nostalgic information, not least of which being the trams on the left of the scene just a few yards in front of Sunderland's beautiful Museum and Library building which was opened in 1879. The addition of the Winter Garden at the rear of the building enabled exhibits such as tropical birds and exotic plants to be seen by local people.

Above: September 1960, and several open spaces indicate the location of recently demolished properties in the heart of the town, soon to be replaced by modern buildings, often clinical in appearance as the age of concrete and and car parks arrived in Sunderland. Many readers may remember that several cleared sites would be used as temporary car parks before work on the new properties commenced. This was a period of transformation as far as Sunderland's housing stock was concerned. Great attempts had been underway since the end of the war to clear the insanitary and overcrowded housing which particularly affected the town centre. Over the following years there would be a tendency for the population to move out of the centre of town and into the newly created housing estates such as the Springwell Farm estate and Thorney Close. Others soon followed, including developments at Downhill, Gilley Law and Town End Farm.

Some new housing developments were constructed near the heart of the town centre - such as the tower blocks and maisonettes at Monkwearmouth and the east end. It was during this period that the pattern of shopping in Britain began to change and the major retail chains started to demand the clean new lines of the sleek modern developments springing up in every town and city centre. Inevitably, this was the start of dramatic changes to the centre of Sunderland, the most notable of which being the construction of the *Walworth Way* - later improved and renamed *The Bridges*. 1960 is remembered in Sunderland as the year that the first smokeless zone was introduced in the area and the first experimental one-way traffic scheme was set in place. On the right of this picture a small sign can be seen which marks the location of Whites Market. By 1967 the market had been swept away to make room for a new market hall with accompanying car park.

Work was in progress on the Hylton Castle Library when this picture was taken. Sunderland can be proud of her record in the provision of libraries throughout her history. A Subscription Library was established on High Street from the second half of the nineteenth century, though it moved to impressive new premises along Fawcett Street in 1878. As early as 1858 local people had access to books at the Public Library next to Sunderland Museum at the Atheneum on Fawcett Street. This proved to be very popular among the inhabitants of the town and by the 1870s it was necessary to build a larger library/museum building off Brough Road. By the turn of the century the stock of books in the library reached 25,000 volumes. In common with the rest of Britain the demand for reading matter was growing at this time and branch libraries were opened at Monkwearmouth, Kayll Road and Hendon. The Hendon branch had the distinction of being the first 'open-access' library in the region.

Tony Wickens/Beamish Museum

Above: This picture dates from May 1953 and is certain to be of interest to railway buffs throughout the area. The photograph features Sunderland Locomotive shed and a group of enthusiasts on the left of the picture can be seen recording the occasion with their own cameras. Thoughts of nostalgia inevitably lead to memories of the age of steam and the giant railway engines that hauled their loads along the busy tracks which covered the region.

Top: This picture was taken in September 1963 and shows the progress being made in the construction of the Sunderland Technical College extension on Chester Road. The works involved building a six-storey teaching block and a 10 storey Student Hostel on the 14 acre site. The work was a small but important part of the post-war educational building programme being carried out in the area. The 1960s are widely regarded as the most dynamic decade in post-war Britain, and 1963 was the most dramatic year in that period. The most tragic and memorable event in 1963 was the assassination of President John F. Kennedy, followed only days later by the murder of the man accused of that crime. Nearer home, the 'Profumo Affair' rocked British politics after a government minister admitted lying to the house of Commons about his relationship with a prostitute, and the "Great Train Robbery" shocked the public with the audacity of the crime. On a lighter note, though it was not considered very amusing at the time, Prince Charles, on an outing from his Gordonstoun School, was spotted by a barmaid ordering a glass of cherry brandy.

Tony Wickens/Beamish Museum

Above: The demolition of the old railway station in Sunderland is featured in this dramatic photograph from 1964. This afforded views of several town centre buildings which had previously been impossible to see, such as the west side of the Town Hall. The railway station had survived wartime bombing on a major scale but was unable to resist the demands of the modern planners who considered the old building unsuitable and ill-equipped to cope with the needs of a busy town centre station. In this picture it is possible to make out the white shape of the end wall of the main part of the station, where once the Station Masters Office, the buffet, (the Bricklayer's Arms) and the Ladies room once stood. The high roof was supported by stylish timber beams - a far cry from the architecture in the modern building which replaced it.

Above right: The rather clinical style the new Sunderland Railway Station is not as elegant as the old Victorian monuments which grace the centre of many other towns and cities, and certainly no match, in terms of appearance at least, for the elegant lines of Monkwearmouth Railway Station.

Work had started in 1964 to demolish the south end of the old railway station. This was followed by the rebuilding of the Athenaeum Street Bridge, a major under-taking in its own right, before the demolition of the north end of the old railway station (the site of which would later be occupied by Littlewoods) and the ultimate construction of the new central railway station. The result is featured in this picture, a rather 'boxy' modern replacement for the old station which really fails to capture the spirit of the 'real' age of the railways.

Right: The interior of a hangar at Sunderland Airport, with major work underway on a twin-engined Dakota aircraft in the centre of the huge expanse of space. The scene looks very 'low-tech' in comparison with modern aircraft maintenance and this image is not helped by the presence of the Standard Pennant van on the right. Of course, this little van, owned by North East Engineering Ltd. of Sunderland and Woolsington airports was entirely in keeping with the transport of the day - this being the earlier part of 1965.

Vaux - Sunderland's favourite brewery

The Vaux family is reputed to have been involved in the Sunderland brewing trade as early as 1805. Certainly, Cuthbert Vaux founded Cuthbert Vaux & Sons in Pemberton Row, close to the river in 1837. It was a small concern with a single drayman, Mr Ferry, whose great-great grand-daughter was working for Vaux in 1964.

In 1875 the business moved to Castle Street where it stayed for twenty years, becoming a private limited company in 1896. By 1900 it employed 200 workers and specialised in the production of India Pale Ale, a "Highly Nourishing Stout".

Maxim Ale was introduced in 1901 to celebrate the gallantry of Major Ernest Vaux during the Boer War. It was probably the first brown ale to be produced as a bottled beer and it was very strong. Because it sent customers to sleep, which was bad for trade, Light Brown Ale was introduced and the strong one was, and still is, named Double Maxim.

The First World War

The war brought many difficulties for the brewing trade: beer duty was increased, price control was implemented, there were restrictions on output and hours of sale. There were also shortages of brewing material and casks, while men, horses and wagons were commandeered by the government. Restrictions on beer strength were particularly frustrating as the government still allowed the sale of higher gravity Irish stout.

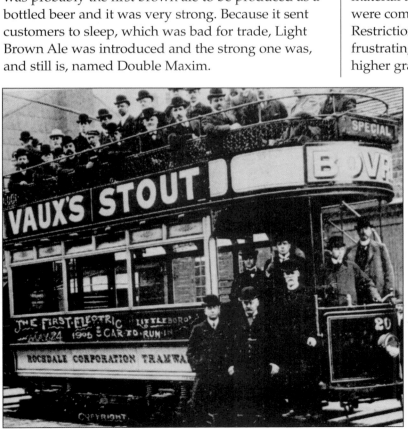

No stout at all was brewed in 1918 because regulations made it 'impossible to produce an article that would give us any credit'. A limited quantity of stronger ales throughout the war gave value for money and output was kept at a reasonable level because Vaux gained the contract to supply beer to army camps in Northumberland and Durham.

Above: Vaux Brewery 1890. The junkyard (top right) was part of the Coopers shop, today the site of the main office block. In the process of construction (top right) is a balcony and buffet bar for the old Avenue Theatre, now the Bottling Hall, purchased by Mr. F.D. Nicholson in 1934 for Vaux. **Left:** *Vaux Stout was famous across the North of England by 1905. This tram was on the first run to Littleborough, Lancs.*

In 1923 Vaux bought John Heslop's Norton Grange Brewery, Norton-on-Tees for use as a distribution centre. In the following year, Wine and Spirit Merchants, J & T Pickering of Spennymoor was acquired, chiefly because it held the Guinness bottling agency.

Ernest Vaux, grandson of the founder died in 1925. In the same year, Vaux bought James Calder & Company

Looking to the future, in October 1915, Vaux bought the Morpeth wine and spirit business run by their agent William Stafford Sanderson for £5,200.

The company expands
In 1919 Frank Nicholson was made managing director for life. To avoid the need for amalgamation or being taken over, he acquired several other breweries, including a controlling interest in their trading partners, Lorimer & Clark. The firm was converted into a limited company in April 1920. By 1926 the share capital had increased to £100,000 and this arrangement between the two companies secured a supply of Scotch beer for Vaux houses.

Above: A picture dating from 1914. The ground floor of the building on the right was the old spirit store. The Casks (left foreground) are wine and spirit casks. Brewer Mr. Aitcheson can be seen in the white coat on the catwalk (in background). Steam engine drays were introduced in 1912 for country deliveries.
Right: Transport vehicles in 1919.

(Brewers) of Alloa and jointly bought Robinson Brothers of Houghton-le-Spring. Vaux took two thirds of the £155,000 of shares on offer. The City Brewery ceased work in 1926 and the houses were divided between Vaux and Calder although Vaux bottled beers were still sold throughout the old Robinson estate.

Associated Breweries Limited
Trade steadily decreased during the 1920s. Frank Nicholson decided on a friendly amalgamation with

the company's rival, North Eastern Breweries Ltd of Sunderland. Both firms were committed to cutting costs and raising standards. In 1927 the two firms became Associated Breweries Ltd with Frank Nicholson as managing director and his son Douglas on the new board.

Nineteen-twenty-nine was Associated Breweries' first complete trading year. In spite of continuing their heavy investment the new company made a profit of £92,755. Slow growth continued despite the economic conditions.

Escape from depression

Associated Breweries continued to buy, their acquisitions between 1934 and 1939 including Berwick Breweries Ltd, Ridley, Cutter & Firth Ltd of the Manor Brewery, best known for their Newcastle Mild Ale sold throughout the coal mining areas of Northumberland, and the Blyth & Tyne Brewery Company Ltd.

In August 1940 the company went public and became known as the Vaux & Associated Breweries Ltd to ensure that the Vaux name would always be attached to the brewing side of the company.

The years of the second war too had brought shortages of brewing materials, weaker beers, beer duty and difficulties with labour and transport. Post-war building restrictions made it impossible to renovate the company's properties. At the 1946 AGM Sir Frank Nicholson thundered that "the beer of Britain is now weaker than in any country in the world."

More mergers led to a long-standing connection with Hepworths. In 1948 the company's financial position was healthy, its capital being valued at over £4,255,000 on the Stock Exchange. In 1950 F H Lamb of Newcastle was taken over to liquidate its stock of whisky.

Sir Frank Nicholson died in December 1952. His association with Vaux stretched back to 1896 and he had chaired the Brewers' Society no less than five times. He was succeeded as Company Chairman by his son Douglas Nicholson.

For the next ten years Vaux looked to Scotland for opportunities to expand. Then, the sixties found Vaux diversifying into hotels, expanding its off-licence trade and moving into sports sponsorship. Building new houses became important and, by 1968 when turnover was just over £23 million the company was spending £1 million a year on new licensed premises. The Swallow Hotel, Newcastle was opened in 1969, the name having been chosen for Vaux hotels by Douglas Nicholson.

Above: Transport vehicles in 1919.
Left: Major Ernest Vaux (front centre).

730 licensed premises. Swallow Hotels had 34 properties with 3420 rooms and were an increasing important part of the Group, run by Deputy Chairman, Peter Catesby. Frank Nicholson, brother of the Chairman, joined the board, having worked for the company since 1981.

During the 80s Vaux responded to changes in the market by producing low alcohol products, using low-temperature technology to preserve the flavour of the beer. They also moved into packaged beer, an important move in the contracting draught market.

Blayney & Company, the off licence chain was acquired and, by 1974, forty one off-licences operated under the Blayney name. Under one of Vaux' sports sponsorships 16,000 pigeons flew in the 1965 Vaux Championships from France to the north of England.

Paul Nicholson, eldest son of Douglas, joined the company board in 1966. In 1971, as joint MD he became the sixth generation of the family to hold the post. In 1972 Wards of Sheffield was taken over.

Change of Name

The company changed its name to Vaux Breweries Ltd in 1973. By this time the company employed 4,766 people and turnover topped £34 million. Expansion and reorganisation of the Castle Street complex continued with the installation of a new, high-speed

bottling plant, a new keg plant and new warehouses. In 1976 Paul Nicholson became Company Chairman on the retirement of his father Douglas.

In 1987 the Group operated two breweries, employed 5,024 people and owned

Vaux and the future

Vaux Breweries remains the country's second-largest independent brewer, with the Castle Street Brewery supplying to managed houses and tenancies. The traditional image of Vaux with its horse-drawn dray belies the fact that in 1991 it became the first UK brewery to earn the quality standard ISO 9002. This prestigious award confirmed the company's commitment to quality. Packaged beer forms a substantial part of the Vaux output.

In 1993 the Group employed 8,200 full time and part time workers while the turnover topped £261 million. The Group Chairman, Sir Paul Nicholson, received his knighthood in the 1993 New Year's Honours List.

Since the establishment of Vaux in the early 19th century its success has rested on hard work and the combination of traditional skills with technical advances and modern management. The lives and histories of many north-eastern families and businesses have been touched by the history of Vaux and the Group is justly proud of its central role in the life of the community as one of the region's leading independent companies.

Above: 1930. Mr. James Agar, Bottling Hall Foreman (centre). ***Left:*** *Frank Douglas Nicholson TD, DL, JP 1905 - 1984. Chairman of Vaux from 1952 to 1976.*

More than a century of service from Alan Duckworth Funeral Directors

More than 100 years ago, Alan Duckworth, the great-great grandfather of the current Alan Duckworth of High Street, ran a business as a builder, joiner and funeral furnisher. His premises were at Holmeside where the company conducted its affairs up to the Second World War.

The founder Alan Duckworth had a son, Jack, whose children grew up to take their places in the firm, the girls, Ivy and Nancy looking after the florist side of the business which had developed over the years whilst the boys, Alan and George looked after the funeral business.

During the war George Duckworth was posted to India and the women in the family, his mother Margaret Jane and sisters, Ivy and Nancy ran the business. From the 1950s funerals and selling flowers have been the firm's sole activities.

In the early days the company made its own coffins and right up to the fifties they still had stables for horses. Now all coffins and caskets are manufactured off site. Funerals are conducted with one hearse and three limousines. A horse-drawn service is still offered but it is hired as required from outside.

In the new premises in High Street the company adapted to new procedures, improved hygienic treatments and embalming

The present owner, another Alan Duckworth has worked in the business for 40 years and officially took it over in the late seventies. Five generations of the family have now been involved in Duckworths funeral services.

Duckworths is the number one funeral directors in the city of Sunderland. Today, business is concentrated mainly there and on Wearside but the company does handle deaths abroad, especially for ex-patriots

The company helps and advises the bereaved in whatever way they can, offering a personal service 24 hours a day and 365 days a year. Staff are trained to look for ways and services that will lift the burden a family suffers in bereavement, either by taking over and relieving its members of responsibility or by following exactly the arrangements that a particular family prefers. Advice is given on the disposal of cremated remains so that there is somewhere for a grieving family to visit, on the kinds of memorial that are available and suitable, and on funeral costs. The average funeral charge in 1892 was one pound, three shillings and sixpence. In 1997 it was £1200. For clients who require it Duckworths provide urns, flowers, catering for funeral guests and anything else that is requested.

> **"THE COMPANY'S MISSION IS ENDEAVOURING TO PROVIDE QUALITY SERVICE TO EVERY FAMILY ON EVERY OCCASION"**

To avoid financial problems making a bereavement worse, Duckworths have provided 'Dignity' a funeral plan that allows clients to arrange and pay for their funeral in advance, saving relatives worry and expense at a time when they are least able to cope. The company is now affiliated with FCI to improve services even further.

*Above: A charming from the 1920s. **Facing page, top:** Jack Duckworth, grandfather of the present owner. **Facing page, bottom:** A 1908 picture of the premises.*

WH Forster (Printers) Ltd - the company born of determination

W.H. Forster (Printers) Ltd, is a growing printing business employing 25 people and operating from premises at Pallion Quay, Sunderland.

The business was founded in 1889, originally located in Brougham Street, in the town centre. It was there that the first electric printing press in Sunderland was installed. For many years the business prospered in a quiet way. However on the death of Mr Forster the business passed to his stepson, Mr Bill Oates and his wife Gladys. Mr & Mrs Oates were mormons and Mr Oates was instrumental in the purchase of land and building of the Mormon Church in Sunderland.

During the late 50s and early 60s the council compulsory purchased Brougham Street for the development of the new town centre. Although the council contributed towards the purchase of alternative premises, Gladys Oates had to sell her shares in the East Timber Co. who traded from Sunderland Dock, and where she had started work after leaving school, eventually working her way through to become a Director and gave this all up to join her husband full time in the business.

Mr Oates had been married previously and at one stage decided to try for a new start in America with his first wife and family in Salt Lake City. Sending his family ahead with the intention of joining them

later. However he did not follow as planned and eventually they divorced. While retaining contact with his family.

After the completion of the move to Villiers Street Gladys Oates took over gradually the day to day running of the company while Bill Oates became more involved with the Mormon Church in Great Britain and eventually rose to the top echelon of the mormon hierarchy.

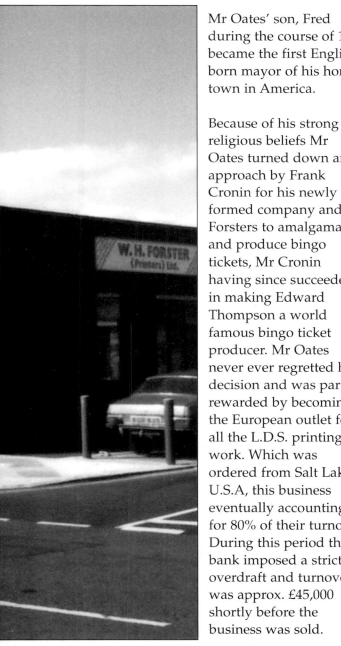

Mr Oates' son, Fred during the course of 1997 became the first English born mayor of his home town in America.

Because of his strong religious beliefs Mr Oates turned down an approach by Frank Cronin for his newly formed company and Forsters to amalgamate and produce bingo tickets, Mr Cronin having since succeeded in making Edward Thompson a world famous bingo ticket producer. Mr Oates never ever regretted his decision and was partly rewarded by becoming the European outlet for all the L.D.S. printing work. Which was ordered from Salt Lake, U.S.A, this business eventually accounting for 80% of their turnover. During this period the bank imposed a strict overdraft and turnover was approx. £45,000 shortly before the business was sold.

In 1982 the business was sold out of the family for £45,000 to Malcolm & Linda Gray. At this time the Oates were planning retirement and turnover and production were not as high as it should have been.

"**FROM THE FIRST ELECTRIC PRINTING PRESS IN SUNDERLAND TO THE LATEST PRINTING TECHNOLOGY AVAILABLE. 1889-1998**"

Mr Malcolm Gray having spent all his working life in the printing industry was able to give fresh energy and impetus to the company. During the next few years things were very difficult, as the mormon contract was withdrawn, equipment had to be replaced and new customers introduced. This proved to be a transitional period, but gradually production and turnover slowly increased with profits used for the purchase of new plant. Business continued to improve and eventually larger premises of 5750 sq. feet were purchased in Nile Street. The move allowed the company to grow, turnover was increasing between 10 - 30% annually, allowing further expansion into the Continuous Forms market. This period being the most financially profitable in the company's history and enabled the purchase of a new site of 69,000 sq. feet. This being the old Doxford Engine Works ship yard site. To retain this identity the new H.Q. are called Doxford Printworks. Initially the move from a comparatively small factory to this huge site was not without its problems, but with the introduction of the latest technological printing processes the site was filled fairly rapidly and the company has managed to maintain 20% increase in annual turnover. Shortly after the move Mrs Gray joined the company full time and has helped the company in the implementation of print management concept. The company produce Thermographic, Lithographic and Continuous print for the print trade market as well as normal business outlets.

The product range encompasses small items from letterheads and business cards through to top quality promotional material - magazines, brochures, leaflets etc... and a direct mail facility is currently being installed.

The latest move will allow continued expansion and the directors look forward confidently increasing the turnover to £4 million in the new millennium.

Left: The Company's premises at Villiers Street.

A reflection on water

The 1980s were declared the 'Decade of Water' by the United Nations' as they realised that water is an increasingly rare and threatened resource. At the same time it is the most vital element in humanity's long fight for survival. We can survive three weeks without food but, after three days without water, we die.

England's first Public Health Act was not introduced until 1848. When it came it was the direct result of a wave of epidemic diseases, principally cholera which scared society into the beginnings of sanitation.

However, another half century passed before it was realised that public health would continue to deteriorate unless something was done about the sanitary conditions in the country's huge areas of industrial slums. The act compelled the provision of a constant piped supply of water, with proper sewage and sanitary facilities to prevent contamination of supplies. Any wastage or fouling of water was punishable by law.

Sunderland and South Shields Water Company

The Sunderland and South Shields Water Company, was formed in 1852 by amalgamating the South Shields, Sunderland and Bishopwearmouth companies. Two years later its administrative area was extended to Jarrow and its vicinity, and a little later still to Whitburn, Hebburn Quay, Houghton le Spring, Newbottle and Shiney Row.

However, in 1869 the company refused to supply the borough of Tynemouth. Tynemouth wanted to escape the Duke of Northumberland's control over water resources. In 1871 the Seaham Harbour Waterworks Company was purchased, followed by Boldon in 1872. Two years later came another refusal, this time to supply water to Gateshead, which was anxious for a better quality of water than that supplied by Newcastle. Had the Sunderland and South Shields Company agreed to supply these two boroughs it could have become one of the country's biggest water companies.

At this time, the idea of publicly owned water services was gaining political favour but the directors in Sunderland refused even to attend a meeting to discuss it.

Between 1846 and 1906 ten new pumping stations were built in Sunderland. Some of these were very elaborate and the cooling ponds at Dalton Pumping Station, were designed by Thomas Hawksley as a formal garden.

The first reservoirs were designed simply to store water taken from springs or pumped from wells and rivers. They began as natural ponds but later were built of stone. As demand increased they became larger and earthen dams were introduced.

Above and left: Ryhope pumping station, pictured before the service reservoir was covered in 1956.
Facing page, top: Ryhope pumping station at the turn of the century, during construction.
Facing page, bottom: A Victorian engine at Ryhope pumping station.

In 1924 New Winning, the very first electrical pumping station, was opened by the company. Then, in 1929, it took over the Castle Eden shaft with its underground pumping station 850 ft below the surface. As demand increased, the company looked to increase its sources of supply and an impounding reservoir was inaugurated at Burnhope in 1937, but the war delayed the laying of the 44 mile pipeline to benefit Sunderland until 1954. Soon after, the Derwent reservoir was constructed by the company in the 1960s and inaugurated in 1967; it had the capacity of 11,000 million gallons, making it one of the biggest in the country.

The war

During the Second World War there were 278 incidents of bomb damage on Sunderland's waterworks. 1941 brought compulsory registration of builders and civil engineering contractors, including water engineers.

Sunderland was divided into 12 zones for the supply of water in emergency. To avoid excessive consumption, water was made

available in accordance with a timetable. Plumbers were in short supply and 'DIY' became the order of the day for bursts whether caused by bombing or frost. Women filled the gap. By 1941, there were five times more women employed in the industry than in 1939.

In 1953 the Ministry of Housing and Local Government offered grants if water undertakings would regroup. The Sunderland and South Shields Company took advantage of the offer, acquiring many smaller undertakings, including the Sunderland RDC and the Washington UDC in 1957.

Within the area were 25,000 people who were supplied with water by the National Coal Board, including Wingate Water Company. The company bought this undertaking along with the rest but found the networks were outdated. The task of renewing them was difficult because of incidents of subsidence caused by mining.

Under government legislation of 1973, the Newcastle and Sunderland Companies worked with the Northumbrian Water Authority to 'plan and control all uses of water in each river catchment area. The Companies worked with one of ten multi-purpose authorities which were both suppliers and regulators to the industry and were responsible for sewage treatment as well as for rivers and water supply.

Suez Lyonnaise des Eaux

This French company concerned itself with the administration of both water and energy sources until 1980 when Jerome Monod became its president. He embarked on an ambitious programme of international development, which included a partnership with the Sunderland and South Shields Water Company in 1988. Four years later, this company amalgamated with Newcastle and Gateshead Water Company to form North East Water.

Northumbrian Water

A further change in name took place in 1996 when Lyonnaise merged North East Water with

Northumbrian Water to create a company which supplies water and sewerage services to 2.6 million people in the North East of England.

Water quality
The Sunderland company had long been concerned about prevention of leakage and pollution of supplies.

In the 19th century water was regarded as pure until some pollution incidents towards the end of the century and the first resident analyst was appointed to the company in 1909. Slow sand filters were initially used but were slow in operation. These were improved after the First World War, but pressure filters weren't introduced to Wearhead, the treatment works for Burnhope until 1959.

After the Second World War, special departments controlled the waste and pollution of water. The company was the first to set up a comprehensive telemetric system for controlling and monitoring its system by computer.

Water Aid
Water Aid is the charity of the British water industry. Founded in 1981, it raises funds to finance projects in Africa and Asia. It acts as a catalyst to help local communities to help themselves in water and sanitation schemes.

Today, 1.4 billion people still lack access to safe water and 2 billion lack access to adequate sanitation, which puts the activities of the companies in the North East in the past into perspective.

Above and left: *Sunderland's Derwent Reservoir. The Derwent Sailing club was opened to members in the same year that it opened.*
Facing page: *HRH Princess Alexandra officially opened Derwent Reservoir on 18th July 1967.*

University of Sunderland - quality education for all

A municipal Technical College was opened near Bishopwearmouth Green, Sunderland in 1901. The decision was stimulated by the possibility of funding under the local Taxation and Customs and Excise Act of 1890. The Galen building, in Green Terrace, original home of the Technical College, was paid for from so-called 'Whiskey Money' at a cost of £27,800.

From the outset the College had much in common with the present University. It enjoyed considerable support from local industry and from people of vision in public life such as Mr Samuel Storey MP and councillor Dr Robert Gordon Bell, the first chairman of the Governors and a leading member of the Higher Education Sub-Committee.

It had close links with other post-elementary education. The Principal, Mr Branford, was Director of Higher Education in the town so he was also responsible for the School of Art and the new Bede Collegiate School. There was also an expressed intention to develop capacity and quality to achieve the status of a University College.

The dynamism of the new College is reflected in the fact that it was the first College in England to introduce the concept of the 'sandwich course'. This enabled engineering apprentices to alternate between College and firm on a six monthly rota and work towards higher qualifications while remaining in employment. This scheme involved 25 engineering firms by 1908. Evening classes were re-structured so that there was progression from two preliminary general years onto two years of more specialist study, a very modern notion. Indeed in 1910 the then Principal, Mr. Victor Mundella wrote "The so-called 'education ladder' is in existence..."

During 1919-1939 the first great surge of expansion took place. The Galen Building was extended between 1922 and 1930 with both private and public funding. In 1939 the industrialist Sir John Priestman opened the Priestman Library with room for 10,000 books. It was fully utilised almost at once and the problem of lack of space continued!

That building was also home to the Mathematics Department and a Mining Department. In 1921-22 also created were Departments of Naval Architecture and Pharmacy. The latter, eventually the largest Pharmacy Department in the country outshining even that of the University of Cambridge, began as a single bench in the Chemistry department! The pioneer was the remarkable scientist Miss Hope C.M. Winch. Growth in quality was reflected in affiliation to the

These developments meant that Sunderland's Technical College was the first in the region with residential accommodation (£5 per week half board). By then there were 1,750 full and part-time students, and the College was the largest of 25 regional colleges. Of the student intake a surprisingly high proportion were Norwegian. That group had grown rapidly from 1946 and reached a peak of 260 in the mid 1960s. By then Sunderland had the largest student body outside Norway itself.

University of Durham in 1930, the establishment of the London University B.Sc. Pharmacy in 1930 and recognition by London University of the College as a centre for its B.Eng. in 1934.

In war-time the College ran special courses for the armed forces and the Ministry of Labour. When normal service was resumed by 1946 the College had 59 full-time staff, 175 part-time assistants, 840 full and part-time students and 1,485 evening class students. New course development in the post-war period included a Department of Housecrafts, recognition of the '......modern woman's realisation that she must have appropriate training if she is to play her part more effectively in her chosen trade, profession or in the home...'

The later 1950s saw further expansion as the College sought the status of College of Advanced Technology. This involved a concentration on advanced work as the two colleges of further education took over most of the non-advanced work. The College was the first educational centre in the region to instal a digital computer ("...The noise means it's calculating..."). From 1959 an ambitious building programme was begun. This culminated in 1964 in the opening of the new complex of buildings on Chester Road by HRH Prince Philip, Duke of Edinburgh.

Above: The Duke of Edinburgh in Sunderland in March 1964, with the Mayor Ald. Mrs J.E Hedley. **Facing page, top:** *The Technical College, Green Terrace, 1901. (Photograph courtesy of Tyne & Wear Museum Services).* **Facing page, bottom:** *The first intake of servicemen for training in radar-controlled gun-firing, taken outside Priestman Building, Green Terrace, between August 1939 and August 1941.* **Below:** *The first students to matriculate as B.Ed students at Sunderland, 1966.*

Diploma in Art and Design in Fine Art. In 1982 Sunderland established its first degree course in Glass design and remains a leading European centre for Glass design and research. In 1988 local motor industry businessman Peter Vardy officially opened the Reg Vardy Art Gallery at Ashburne, in honour of his father.

The Training College opened in 1908 with 70 students, male and female, and tuition fees of £10 per annum. Staff included a Sergeant Major to teach 'Swedish Drill' and a 'Mistress of Method'. In 1922 students moved into the grand Langham Tower in Ryhope Road (bought by the Corporation for £8000). At the same time the College became a women-only college, which it remained until 1959. The post-Second World War era saw considerable expansion with more hostel places in Park House and Westfield Hall and provision of gymnastics and drama facilities in Bede Tower. Under its last Principal Mr H Armstrong James, the Training College reached its zenith with 820 students and 80 staff.

Sunderland Polytechnic was created from 1st January 1969, with a new teacher training Department of Education established in the same year. The Polytechnic was among the first three of the thirty national institutions, which were to concentrate on courses of a professional or vocational nature and develop part-time provision.

The Polytechnic brought together the Technical College with two other institutions which had played a significant role in the town; the School of Art and Sunderland Training College.

A School of Art was established in 1901. Classes were run in rooms in the Town Hall. Indeed there was a formal request that students be allowed to use the main entrance because 'the young ladies complained that they were brought in unpleasant contact with the dirty people frequenting the Health Department!'. As well as a fine art curriculum the College also ran classes in painting and decorating, stone and wood carving, photography, millinery and dressmaking. The industrial classes grew rapidly as the employers paid the fees of many of the students. In 1934 the College of Arts and Crafts moved to new accommodation in Ashburne House, donated by T W Backhouse. Student numbers grew over 1000 by 1960. In 1963 the re-designated College of Art began to offer the degree-equivalent

By 1968 the College ran the first interdisciplinary undergraduate degree programme outside the University sector (B.Sc. Materials Science). In 1973 it mounted the first part-time in-service B.Ed in the country. By 1980 the student body had leapt to 2294 full-time and sandwich students, 1446 part-time students and 2000 short course attenders.

The first Sunderland Honorary Fellowships were awarded in 1975 to Dame Flora Robson DBE, Sir Montague Finniston and Brendan Foster. Since then other Honorary Awards have been conferred upon people as diverse as the opera singer Thomas Allen, the

Olympic athlete Steve Cram, the former Bishop of Durham The Rt. Rev David Jenkins, the musician Dave Stewart and the BBC broadcaster Kate Adie, as well as distinguished scientists, academics and industrialists. In 1990 Dr Anne Wright was appointed Rector at Sunderland. She then became the first female Vice-Chancellor of an English university when the Polytechnic gained University status in the government education reforms in 1992. In the same year HM The Queen granted Sunderland city status to mark her 40th year on the throne.

In 1993 HM The Queen and HRH The Duke of Edinburgh visited Sunderland and the University to celebrate. Her Majesty met University staff and saw plans for the flagship St. Peter's Campus development. St. Peter's Campus brings a new era to Sunderland. The Campus, designed by architect Tony McGuirk of Building Design Partnership, with Sunderland's glass and shipping heritage in mind, is a second base for a University of 15,000 students. Sunderland Business School opened here in 1994, the spectacular new School of Computing & Information Systems followed two years later. The Royal link continues. It was HRH The Prince of Wales who came in April 1996 to lay a foundation stone to mark the official opening of the whole Campus.

The Campus has strong Northern connections and plays a real regional role. The Catherine Cookson Reading Room, a reflective place for quiet study, honours the local author and benefactor. The 400-seater Sir Tom Cowie Lecture Theatre, named after the Sunderland businessman who supported the development of its state-of-the-art audio visual facilities, has been the venue for an international conferences and community musical concerts, as well as student lectures.

Into the 21st century, the University of Sunderland, founded on strong community roots and partnerships with local business people and visionaries, looks forward to a great new era - an era of communications technology, glass and creative artistry and the continuing regeneration of Sunderland and the North East for many years to come.

Above: Vice-Chancellor Dr Anne Wright CBE with HM The Queen, 1993.

Facing page, top: Arts Students in Ashburne house in the early 1960s.

Facing page, bottom: Sunderland Training College students 1933.

Thanks are due to Stuart Miller for compiling the history of the University for this article.

City of Sunderland College - planning for the future

The roots of today's City of Sunderland College go back to the post-War years when educationalists, both national and local, began to consider how best to prepare young people for a fast-changing, technological future.

Monkwearmouth College and West Park College, the forerunner of Wearside College, were established in 1962 when Sunderland Technical College became an institution of higher education, as Sunderland Polytechnic - now the University of Sunderland.

Described by the Sunderland Echo as "ultra modern", the new college - now the Tunstall Centre of City of Sunderland College - offered industrial and technical training for 1,800 students. In 1972 it was officially opened by Education Secretary Margaret Thatcher who, during her visit, bemoaned the lack of jobs for graduates.

Above: A 1970s view of Wearside College, now City of Sunderland College's Tunstall Centre.
Left: The College's Bede Centre, formerly Bede School.
Below: Swan Street Centre, formerly Monkwearmouth Grammar School.

The newly-created further education institutions took on the former technical college's lower level craft and technician courses, with Monkwearmouth assuming responsibility for the emergent service sector, in former grammar school premises at Swan Street.

Business, including wide-ranging secretarial programmes, and general studies were first in to the new centre and a tower block was created to provide purpose-built premises for food technology, baking, tailoring, nursing and the like.

Meanwhile, West Park offered courses to train workers for the engineering and construction industries. In 1971, these programmes were transferred to a brand new £1 million centre - Wearside College of Further Education.

NORTHEAST PRESS LIMITED, SUNDERLAND ECHO

At this stage, the two colleges were starkly different, with male-dominated Wearside specialising in training for the traditional heavy industries and Monkwearmouth, which had equal numbers of young women and men, developing as a general education college which also provided for the new service industries.

The popularity of care courses, nursery nursing, hotel & catering and, increasingly, computing, mirrored the skills needs of local industries and demand from individual students, who were fortunate to benefit from the local authority's forward-looking attitude towards non-mandatory grants.

Monkwearmouth's substantial growth during the 1970s reflected changes in society at large, with a dramatic increase in the number of girls progressing to further education as well as a trend towards older women returning to education as mature students, many of whom went on to complete their studies at Sunderland Polytechnic.

Above: Margaret Thatcher, then Education Secretary, officially opened Wearside College in 1972.
Right: The College's Hylton Centre.

As the college grew it expanded into various other accommodation and, in 1987, took over the former St Thomas Aquinas School premises, now the college's Hylton Centre.

As the region's traditional industries declined during the 70s and 80s, the challenges for Wearside College were rather different to those of Monkwearmouth.

There was a major shift in the college's operation, with mining courses disappearing and shipbuilding reduced to a small fraction of its former prominence.

Wearside College began to provide training for the modern industries which replaced them and extended its links to other areas of business.

Notably, its support for Nissan Motor Manufacturing (UK) Ltd was recognised by a Department of Trade & Industry award in 1990.

Left: Gerry Milton, ex Monkwearmouth College Principal and Don Chroston, ex Chairman of Monkwearmouth College Board of Governors laying the foundation stone for Monkwearmouth College's Shiney Row Centre.
Below: Neil Kinnock, then Leader of the Opposition, opened Monkwearmouth College's Shiney Row Centre in June 1990.

At the same time, Wearside's gender balance began to alter as it forged a partnership with the Washington-based Bridge women's initiative to help hundreds of women who would not normally attend college gain confidence and tackle further education and, in some cases, higher education courses.

In September 1989, Monkwearmouth and Wearside Colleges became tertiary colleges and, between them, began to provide most of Sunderland's post-16 public sector education.

Wearside College gained a second base in Durham Road, Sunderland, in the former Bede School and Monkwearmouth acquired the former Shiney Row School. Wearside was given additional responsibility for A level courses and some general vocational education for the south of Sunderland. Meanwhile, Monkwearmouth expanded its A level and general vocational provision in the north and west of the city.

The local papers quickly dubbed Shiney Row Centre the "fame school" in recognition of its flourishing creative arts courses. In reality, the college encouraged a broad-based arts approach, training teachers and therapists as well as performers.

There was further change ahead in April 1993, when the further education sector ceased to be under local authority control. Both colleges became State-supported independent corporations and began to receive funding direct from central government through the Further Education Funding Council. Despite this shift in status, both colleges retained their close links with the local authority.

The two colleges came full circle in August 1996, joined once more in a single institution, when they merged under the leadership of Ian Todd, following the retirement of Monkwearmouth and Wearside principals, Gerald Milton and Alan Cass.

Now, as the UK's fifth largest further education institution, City of Sunderland College continues to support Wearsiders of all ages as they take up the challenges of an increasingly technological world. The college's commitment to advanced manufacturing, and its emphasis on science and technology, is matched by an equally strong commitment to reaching out into the community.

Within the next few years City of Sunderland College aims to have four centres of excellence, serving all of Wearside. They will comprise the Hylton Centre in the north, Shiney Row and Bede to the south and, to complete the quartet, an exciting new centre at Washington.

Above: Alan Cass, former Principal, Wearside College hands over to Ian Todd, Principal, City of Sunderland College on the new College's first day.
Left: Monkwearmouth College's Shiney Row Centre.

Over a century of quality education

Argyle House, Sunderland's oldest independent school can trace its history back to March 1884. It is thought to have been named after Argyle House in Argyle Square.

It was originally a day and boarding school, founded by James Hanna. Ten years later, it moved from Argyle Square to St George's Square where it continued to flourish. More than 1,000 pupils passed through the doors of the school before the outbreak of the First World War.

Many former pupils served with distinction during the war, with one in particular, 2nd Lieut. Kenneth Storey being awarded the Military Cross.

Towards the end of 1915, the school became mixed with the introduction of a new commercial department, which lasted until 1921. At this time, the school took in a record number of 122 pupils in one year.

When Mr Hanna died in 1924, his son, James, took over the headship and ran the school with the help of assistant headmaster, James Gash.

James Hanna died in 1937, leaving the school in the capable hands of his three daughters who all taught at the school. This was a traumatic time for most people with the threat of war looming. Indeed, in 1943 the school was virtually destroyed during a bombing raid, forcing the school to move premises again to Thornhill Park.

The school faced many problems during the following years, including shortages of school equipment and the nationwide problem of rationing.

Above: *This picture dates from the turn of the century and shows two of the Hanna sisters with the whole school.*
Left: *A House Cricket Team c1953. Today's headmaster is 2nd right on the front row.*

However, after the war, conditions gradually improved, under the headship of talented men, who included J.E. Pattison and G. 'Sunny' Ray.

The last Miss Hanna died in 1968 and the school was bought a year later by a former pupil and staff member, Mr J.N. Johnson, who finally took over as headmaster in 1972; in 1976 the school moved further along the road to its present location 19/20 Thornhill Park.

Despite the rise and fall of pupil numbers, over the years the school has survived and flourished, which may have something to do with the school motto, 'Work Conquers All'.

Serving the locality and even further afield, the school takes in pupils from all walks of life, from all over the north east of England. Children are taught to respect their peers and elders, and to have ambition for their futures. Also, it is school policy to instill good manners and discipline.

The school became co-educational in 1995, introducing girls for the first time since World War I. Although this inevitably meant great change for the school, in true style, it has weathered any problems this might have caused.

Argyle House remains, today, one of the area's most popular schools and has a bright future. The teachers know all their pupils and parents by name, which maintains the feeling of familiarity and homeliness and, with the determination to ensure that the average child does better, the school's future does indeed look promising.

Above: Sports day 1952 sees a group of boys about to set off in a race.
Left: This was the first time the school had a trip overseas- also believed to have been the first time a Sunderland school went abroad.

Corning - from the Wear to the world

Glassmaking developed and subsequently declined in the north east over the last century and a half. During this century only two major glassmaking firms on Wearside survived, Turnbulls and Joblings. Turnbulls was forced to close in 1953 and Joblings abandoned the production of lead glass in 1960.

Joblings were able to continue in business because they had acquired the sole rights in this country to the manufacture of heat-resistant Pyrex table wares. This type of glass had been invented by the American firm of Corning which took over Joblings in 1973.

Corning Limited is proud of its contribution to the Sunderland community. It is a wholly-owned subsidiary of Corning International Corporation of the US and is carrying on a tradition of glassmaking that has existed along the banks of the Wear for centuries.

The history of the present company goes back to 1886 when James Augustus Jobling, a Newcastle industrialist and supplier of glass-making chemicals took over one of the existing firms and took his nephew, Ernest Jobling-Purser into business with him. Ernest was the man responsible for its subsequent growth.

Before 1914 the majority of laboratory glass was made in Germany. Corning Glass Works had initially developed a glass for railway signal lanterns that was thermal shock resistant and one for battery jars that had chemical resistance.

In 1912 they developed a glass combining the best properties of both, calling it Nonex. In 1915 they demonstrated that this type of glass was satisfactory for baking and called it Pyrex. In 1921 as head of the company, Ernest Jobling-Purser secured from Corning, the above mentioned rights in Pyrex.

The first Pyrex brand products made at the Wear Glass Works the following year were for household use and included casseroles. The new glass, known as borosilicate, was thermally strong and robust. It was later used to make laboratory and industrial ware. The stage was set for further development and expansion. Today the company products are sold in more than 120 world markets and about half of these export sales now come from the countries of Europe.

Production in Sunderland was divided into Pressware and Blownware. Pressware products range from cups to casseroles in both clear and opaque heat resistant glass which are bought by housewives in 94 customer countries as well as the UK. 1975 brought a Queen's Award for Export Achievement.

The Blownware Department used to produce glass from three large oil-fired tanks and form it into a wide of shapes and sizes. Blownware production continues with products ranging from small watch glasses and laboratory beakers to large flasks for chemical and process plant use. The highly skilled hand blowers make about 1,000 different items a year and industrial glass products made in Sunderland are distributed worldwide.

The Science Products division established a factory at Pallion which was concerned with making, manipulating and processing glass materials supplied by the Blownware Department. The majority of the finished products were for the chemical and process plant industries. They ranged from components weighing less than half an ounce to plant items with a glass weight in excess of 100lbs and at its height the factory produced over three million items a year.

The Wear Glass Works has long been one of the mainstays of employment in Sunderland. Originally it was just one of many local glassworks but with the sad news of the closure in 1997 of a local firm producing elegant stained glass, it has outlived them all. However, Corning Limited has expanded its activities from the Wear to the world and the company is optimistic for the future, intending to continue as an asset both to the local community and the country.

Facing page, top: The Joinery Workshop.
Facing page, bottom: The Mould Room.
Above: Members of the Maintenance team take a break.
Left and below: Brothers Norman and Jimmy Davidson in action.

The business founded on a bet

The firm of Edward Thompson was started in 1867 because a go-ahead young businessman won a bet at horse racing. The young man was Edward Thompson, the firm's founder. He went to a race meeting, picked what he thought would be the winner, and then judiciously laid odds on the horse.

The result was that he won £60 which was considerably more valuable in 1867 than it would be today. Edward Thompson added his winnings to his life savings and bought property in Sunderland.

He started as a printer and, by dint of hard work, built up a stationery business as well. Mr Thompson had no children so the business eventually passed to his nephew,

George Curren. Curren was a bachelor, so the business next passed to his nephews George Edmonds, and John Louis Cronin who entered the business after his return from the trenches in 1918.

John Louis eventually became sole owner and took an active part in the business until his death in 1980, but he was succeeded as Managing Director in 1956 by the middle one of his three sons,

Frank, who had joined the company in 1953 after his national service in the RAF.

In 1959, the stationery shop, at that time in South Street and Walworth Street found a mounting demand for the bingo tickets which they sold. The firm was retailing tombola cards for a firm in Ipswich who told Mr Cronin at one point that they could only let Thompsons have 3,000 books a month. The company at that time was selling 10,000 a month with ease. They wondered whether it would be a good idea to print their own, decided to do so and have never looked back. It seemed a fitting way to prosper for a firm that was initially financed by a bet on a horse.

After the bingo cards had been compiled with the aid of the firm's 'computations system' they were set out in type form and printed in sheets.

Above: John Louis Cronin (standing) with his mother, two sisters and brother, Donal in 1919. He took over the business from George Curren, along with his cousin, George Edmonds.
Left: Sunderland High Street at the turn of the century. At the far right hand side of the picture, Edward Thompson's premises can be seen. The young boy looking in the window had obviously seen something that caught his eye.
Top left: George Curren, nephew of Edward Thompson, who was a bachelor and and inherited the business from his uncle.

Due to expansion a second factory went up in 1965. Soon there were no fewer than thirteen Heidelberg 10x15 inch platens and five double crown cylinders, most of them engaged in producing up to 50,000,000 tickets weekly, consuming nearly 50 tons of paper. By now Thompsons had a staff of 300 who enjoyed ideal working conditions that included bonus schemes and piped music.

The sheets were cut into strips, each strip containing six cards. Machines then stitched the strips together into book form. The books were packed, labelled and added to the always diminishing piles in the firm's stockroom. The firm's proud boast was 'Order one day and the cards arrive the next!'

From printing bingo cards the firm broadened its scope to make all the equipment that went with playing bingo. They offered a 'bespoke bingo service' covering advice, equipment manufacture, installation and the supply of bingo tickets.

A most important part of the new business process was delivering the goods on time. Edward Thompsons gave this matter their full attention. On every day of the week vans came and went with the millions of tickets printed at the factory. The fleet of vans, a four-tonner, two two-tonners, two one-tonners and three minis, delivered all over the British Isles

"AS LONG AS THE CRY OF 'BINGO!' OR 'HOUSE!' CAN BE HEARD IN BRITAIN, THOMPSON'S WILL BE KEPT BUSY."

Centenary year was celebrated by a staff dinner dance which attracted 530 guests at the Top Rank Suite in Sunderland, a tradition which continues to the present day, with almost 1,000 people celebrating at the 1998 dinner dance.

Mr Cronin had ample faith in the future. The home market stretched from the Orkneys to Jersey, the company vans delivered all over Britain and export chances were developing. The company still owned a shop in the High Street that functioned as a stationers and Catholic repository. (The Cronin family are Roman Catholics, John Louis' brother was a Parish Priest and his younger son, James Donal is a priest with the Mill Hill Society, and served with the African Foreign Mission).

1970 brought the investment of a further £250,000 for more accommodation. For some time the sheer volume of production had stretched the resources of the single storey factory. Stocks of 400 million bingo

Above: Workers checking bingo tickets in the 1960s.

tickets at any one time presented a big enough space problem without space for printing and collating the tickets, and the checking systems that were necessary to ensure the tickets were numbered correctly. One mistake could have ruined the firm's reputation with the major chains of bingo halls.

In 1975 the company bought the old Echo Office premises in West Wear Street, and in 1981 opened it as a match factory, producing advertising bookmatches for the UK and Europe. Today it is the only match manufacturer in the United Kingdom.

Also in 1981 the Group bought Hendon Paper Mill from Domtar, a Canadian papermaking company. Domtar had closed down the mill eleven months previously with the loss of 600 jobs. Within six months the mill was back in business, producing 100% recycled paper, keeping alive a tradition of papermaking in Sunderland, started even before St. Bede sat on the bank of the River Wear in 674AD, translating the Bible.

As long as the cry of 'Bingo!' or 'House!' can be heard in Britain - and who will be brave enough to say when it will end? -Thompsons will be kept busy. However, even if the bottom went out of the bingo market tomorrow, they are happy in the knowledge that they have the staff, equipment and the 'know how' to adapt to virtually any other kind of printing job. Their factory includes all the latest printing machinery, automatic silk screen process, platemaking, letterpress, foil printing and thermography, as well as a £1,000,000 electronic imaging machine.

With such a wealth of experience behind it, the company continues to expand from the small printing company with seven staff which Frank Cronin took over in 1956, to a group of companies which now employs over 700 and which exports to over 57 countries throughout the world.

The group has evolved to what it is today due to the entrepreneurial skills of Frank Cronin and the hard work and loyalty of the people who have worked with him over the years, many of whom have been with the company since the 1960s. To date, over 85 members of staff have received a gold watch as a 'thank you' for 25 years service with the company.

The expansion continues with a new factory envisaged for Richmond Street during 1998, and an envelope manufacturing plant planned in the near future.

Above and left: *The Edward Thompson premises today, a far cry from the tiny shop on Sunderland High Street at the turn of the century.*

Blacklock's - the jewel in Sunderland's crown

The origins of the well known Sunderland company, Blacklock Jewellers go back to over a century and a half ago and to the docks of the Tyne. Robert Blacklock began his working life as a shipwright, in a time when the north east of England had a thriving shipping community.

The early days

It was, then, an unusual step for the young man to open his own shop as a pawnbroker and jeweller in Bedford Street, Sunderland. It proved in time to be a good move on Robert's part. His business became well known in the area and his services were called upon time and time again.

Before long, Robert's son joined the business and then his grandson. It has been this way ever since, with five generations of the same family having run the business. The shop remained at the Bedford Street premises until the turn of the century when it moved to Bridge Street and then to Waterloo Place in 1962.

The depression

Between the wars the company faced the worldwide problem of the depression. People had

little or no money to spend on anything frivolous and it was at that time that Ralph Hope Blacklock, the present senior partner's grandfather was diagnosed as having tuberculosis and had to retire early.

He moved to Switzerland to recover, leaving his son, Kenneth Ellis, who was still at school at the time, to take over. It was a difficult time for the young lad but in true family spirit he kept the business going.

The Second World war

When Kenneth's father began to recover from his illness he was called back to the shop when the Second World War broke out and Kenneth enlisted in the army.

Again the company faced a troublesome time. Very little business was done and although the management were able to keep the shop afloat, it was hardly profitable.

Above: Bridge Street at the turn of the century. The company moved here from Bedford street.
Left: Ralph Hope Blacklock striking a very elegant pose. This photograph dates from before World War I when the company was at Bridge Street.

However, when peace returned the company found itself with plenty of clients who wanted the things that were denied them during the war. The company began to specialise in high quality jewellery and was along those lines that the company continued.

The move to Waterloo Place in 1962 proved to be a great success and in 1981 the family were able to open new a outlet in Durham.

There have been times when the company has been 'run off its feet', which on one occasion could have cost the company a considerable amount of money. At an auction in 1973 the buyer for the company saw an Arab Ceremonial Dagger and picked it up for £1000. It had a beautiful gold handle which was set with precious gems.

> **"AFTER WORLD WAR II, THE COMPANY FOUND ITSELF WITH PLENTY OF CLIENTS WHO WANTED WHAT HAD BEEN DENIED THEM FOR SO LONG."**

The company sent a press release and displayed it in the window for £1250. There was a considerable amount of public and press interest but it inexplicably failed to sell.

Deciding to cut its losses, the company sent the dagger to be melted down only to receive a cheque for £3000 days later. Nobody had realised that the belt that came with the dagger was made from 18ct gold wire!

And now....
Today, the company mainly caters for the wealthier end of the market with most of their clients being white collar workers and professional men and women.

The mainstay of their business is beautiful traditional jewellery and top quality watches and gifts, that will literally last a lifetime. Many of their goods are passed down through families.

Being expert dealers in diamond, gold and gem set jewellery, people come to the company for advice, knowing that they will receive only the very best service. With a Fellow of the Gemmological Association and a holder of a Diamond Diploma on the staff, the company's pride in its abilities is well founded.

To the future
At the moment the company is involved in the development of a jeweller.'s computer system and is in the process of setting up on the internet.

In years gone by, the future of this company was never certain in that it had to face all the hardships of the depression and both World Wars but with the quality of its goods and service its future now looks rewarding.

Left: A 1909 invoice for a local customer, Adam Tindle who bought his goods and was able to pay for them over a twelve month period.

Coutts & Findlater - shopfitters of quality

Coutts & Findlater was established in 1918 by Mr Coutts. He began by making small cabinets and carrying out furniture repairs. He quickly built up a reputation for his fine craftsmanship and by 1924 he was able to form a limited company, Coutts Furniture Limited. Mr Coutt's object was to carry on in the manufacture of cabinets as well as diversifying into other furniture. He also began work as an interior shop fitter and furniture dealer. There were many more other avenues he explored such as decorating, carving, gilding, manufacturing mouldings and making picture frames. The firm was also ready and willing to carry out any other services connected with its line of business.

During the years up until 1930 the company was engaged mainly in the manufacture of hand made furniture, wood mantels, interior shopfittings and the restoration of antique furniture. Because of the good reputation for quality, the firm was often called upon to make church furniture and wood carvings.

Mr Coutts had a small army of highly skilled craftsmen and also trained a number of apprentices, who served seven years at a time. It was during 1930 that Mr Findlater bought shares in the firm and the name was changed to the current Coutts and Findlater. Mr Findlater was experienced in shop front design and manufacture and the firm began a natural progression into this field, carrying out many high quality projects in the pre-war period. The company advertised itself as Bank, Office & Shopfitters. It was a ground breaking time, a period of hard work and team spirit. The basic material used was wood and the work was labour intensive.

Occasionally steel and bronze were used but this proved, on the whole, too expensive for most of the smaller retailers.

With the outbreak of World War II came government restrictions on buildings. Shopfitting and furniture making were discontinued, whilst the company was redirected into work for the war effort, making ship's deck houses and binnacles. Later, it began repairing bomb damaged furniture and the manufacture of black out shutters for military establishments. The factory itself was bombed and severely damaged during the war and shortly after, Mr Findlater retired.

The post war years were very difficult for the firm, due to a shortage of materials and the ongoing restrictions on all building work and it was small jobs, although not very interesting which kept the company going. Restrictions were finally lifted and the company applied for a licence to rebuild the factory which had been damaged in a bombing raid. It was agreed and

work began in 1950. This period also meant that the company could return to shopfitting and it began to receive work from local traders for bomb damage repairs and replacements. Soon, the company found it was having trouble keeping up with demand and had to expand its workforce.

The firm continued in this vein, expanding rapidly in the 1960s with the arrival of shopping precincts and centres springing up everywhere. The factory was extended once more and the machine shop was re-equipped.

Then came the arrival of power tools. Once, a job that traditionally took months could now be completed in weeks. This meant that more work had to be found and the company expanded into other areas to compensate. Banks, hotels, pubs, clubs and ships were just some of the contracts taken on and to this day, the firm will literally fit out anywhere.

New techniques have swept the industry, mainly with the introduction of Computer Aided Manufacture (CAM) and although this has been a breakthrough, the building trade has been affected by the recession since 1989 and the company has had to adjust its organisation to meet the new demands recession imposes. But there is more confidence about for the future and Coutts & Findlater Ltd look forward to the new millennium and great things for the north of England.

Above: A display stand at a 1930 exhibition. This was just after Mr Findlater had joined the company.
Left: An ice-cream parlour fitted by Coutts & Findlater during the 1930s.
Facing page, top: This namestyle was adopted in 1930.
Facing page, bottom: The offices, shop and factory in the 1930s.

Fred Williamson & Sons Ltd - over a century of service to the wallpaper industry

This company of specialist wholesale merchants to the decorating trade, is the largest independent firm in the North East of England, with branches also in Newcastle and Middlesbrough and with the most comprehensive range of products available from one source.

Its roots are a rather different story. In 1874 Frederick Williamson as a young man who was apprenticed with Robert Airey, a well known clock and watch maker in Sunderland. Fred thought that he had found his career but after eighteen months into his apprenticeship, Mr Airey died, leaving the young man without a job. He had no choice but to find another trade. After searching around, doing odd jobs here and there he finally found another indenture with John Coates, training to be a Paperhanger and Upholsterer. In those days, this was considered to be one trade.

An enterprising man, Fred began trading on his own soon after completing his novitiate and by 1884, he had opened his own wallpaper shop at Number 2, Dundas Street, Monkwearmouth. He worked alongside his wife, who in between raising the couple's six children, helped him in the shop. Two of the six children were sons, Fred and Harry, both of whom later became directors of the firm.

The company grew over the following decade until 1906 when it had made a sufficient impression on The

Above: An invoice from the 1950s.
Above left: Frederick Williamson senior, founder of the area's largest independent firm of wholesale decorators merchants. He died in 1937.
Below: The newly renovated shop front at 2/3 Dundas Street in 1923.

Wallpaper Manufacturers of Manchester (now the well known company, Crown Wallcoverings Ltd) that they gave Fred merchant's terms, allowing him to resell their wallpaper to other decorators and retailers.

The sons of Frederick Williamson served their apprenticeships as painters and paperhangers and this line of business led the company forwards until the 1920s, when the company decided to concentrate on wholesale supply to the painting trade. In 1929 the firm was incorporated as a Private Limited Company, with the shares being allotted to Fred Williamson and his two sons. The minute book shows that the firm sustained a steady but reliable growth until the outbreak of war in 1939, when wallpaper and paint factories were converted to produce weapons and tools for war. Home decorating was an unnecessary luxury, even distemper and whitening were in short supply.

It was a difficult time for the firm although within two years of the war ending, the firm had expanded within its premises, taking on a new director, Randle Oliver, who had been with the RAF for four years. He took over the wallpaper sales.

He eventually took over the business in 1961 when the Williamson brothers decided to retire, selling Randle and his wife their shares. The Olivers' two sons, Anthony and Christopher joined the firm in 1971 and 1972 and are now joint Managing Directors.

The firm grew over the ensuing years with another breakthrough coming in 1981 with the firm's appointment as Regional Distributors of Crown Wallcoverings. For some time, the company had been outgrowing its home at Dundas Street and the directors had been searching the area for more suitable premises. It was in 1984, after exactly one hundred years in Dundas Street, that the firm moved to a new location, a 20,000 sq.ft. warehouse in Roker Avenue, which had previously housed British Ropes.

During that same year, Randle Oliver was appointed National Chairman of the Builders Merchants Federation, followed five years later by his selection as National President of the British Association of Wallcoverings Merchants. In 1986 computers were installed for the first time, for the management of accounts and stock.

Nowadays, the company's customer base is widening all the time. It has representatives calling on clients from Berwick on Tweed in the north, Scarborough in the south and Cumbria in the west.

It has a fleet of lorries who make daily deliveries to decorators, retail shops, DIY outlets and local authorities. With a history such as is behind this company, it has built up a reputation for service and product assortment that is second to none.

Above: The premises at Dundas Street prior to 1923 renovations.
Left: The staff of Fred Williamson & Sons in 1960s. Randle Oliver (the current Chairman) is in the centre of the picture.

More than a century of security for fishermen from Sunderland Marine Mutual Insurance Co Ltd

Sunderland Marine Mutual Insurance Company Limited, whose original name was the Total Loss Mutual Steamship Insurance Company, was formed in 1882 by a number of Sunderland shipowners, prominent amongst whom was one Ralph Hudson. His family firm, R. Hudson & Sons, shipowners brokers and merchants had owned ships registered in Sunderland for more than 200 years. The port of Sunderland at the time of the formation of the Company was one of the biggest and busiest seaports in the British Isles.

The Company was started to meet the insurance needs of increasing shipping in and out of the port but at the very time of the Company's formation there was a decline in this growth. However the Company expanded because it spread its business over the country and it foresaw the potential of the fishing industry.

It established itself as a specialist in the insurance of fishing vessels.

Almost 120 years ago the founder members sat at a meeting to consider the first claim of £1,600 for the total loss of the steamship 'Advance'. They would have been astounded if they could have seen the amounts the Company deals in today. £2m is the largest single claim on the Company to date.

The Company prospered during the sustained boom in the British fishing industry that occurred during the years 1900 - 1913. Records show 300 vessels were insured at the beginning of this period - 1500 vessels at the close.

The membership of the Company declined steadily during the next 35 years. The reasons for this were various but the most immediate and important was the effect upon the fishing industry of the world-wide economic depression of the 1920s and 1930s.

Above: *Sunderland's busy fish quay at the turn of the century.*
Left: *This sturgeon was a rare catch for North Shields fishing folk.*

The history of the Company during the Second World War was largely a repeat of the First World War. For the second time in 25 years large numbers of fishing vessels and tugs were requisitioned by the Government for use as mine-sweepers, patrol boats and auxiliary naval craft. At the outbreak of the war the Company was insuring some 348 vessels. Many craft became worn out during the six years of war and owing to restrictions were not replaced. Many others were lost on war service. When the war ended in 1945 the membership had been reduced to 248 vessels.

In the early 1950's diesel power began to replace the old steam driven vessels and the Board of the

Above: *John Ness, Secretary of the Total Loss Company in Sunderland from 1897-1921.*
Right: *The Pilot Jack, an all-sail trawler being towed out to the fishing grounds by tug at the turn of the century.*
Below: *A large catch of herring. The wearing of bowler hats indicated the foremen.*

Company resolved to endeavour to capture a share of this market which included the larger middle and near water trawlers as well as the rapidly expanding fleet of diesel powered inshore fishing vessels.

To enable the Company to deal efficiently with the increasing membership a move was made from West Sunniside to larger premises at The Esplanade which it occupies today. By 1974 the Company's determined efforts to increase business had resulted in a total of 426 vessels being insured. Of greater significance was the fact that the total sums insured had increased to nearly £12m in contrast with the £1.25m which were insured in 1955.

Above: A stranded trawler having securing lines attached prior to being refloated.
Above left: This trawler was successfully salvaged after being washed ashore in the high spring tide, and carried to safety by low-loader.
Below: The Eppleton Hall, a Sunderland paddle tug pictured on the Wear. Paddle tugs could turn on a sixpence and worked until the 1960s.

At the end of 1974 the Company took a most important step by effectively merging with the marine underwriting firm of Salvus Bain and Arnott Ltd, also of Sunderland, which firm also specialised in the insurance of fishing vessels. The latter was a company once owned by one Moffitt Outhwaite whose father had been Secretary of the Company until his death in 1945 after some 40 years of service with the Company. The name was subsequently changed to Salvus Bain (Management) Ltd, now the Managers of Sunderland Marine.

Right: The Golden Strand, a 63ft inshore trawler.
Below: A result of the perils faced by fishermen at sea, Sunderland Marine occupy their business in dealing with the casualties and emergencies that arise.

> ## "IN 1986 THERE WAS A MOVE INTO THE FISH FARMING INDUSTRY WITH THE FORMATION OF AQUACULTURE"

When Sunderland Marine was formed as a Mutual Company, one of the principle criteria was that of service to vessel owners in times of

need. The quality of service and expertise was expanded overseas in 1979 when the Directors agreed to accept Reinsurance business from Holland. Further developments continued in Commonwealth countries including Australia, New Zealand and Canada and in 1986 the Company was invited to become involved in the U.S.A. market where the same quality of risk selection and service was carried forward.

This page: *A fishing vessel which sank in a harbour being raised by direct crane lift.*

A further diversification occurred when the decision was made to become involved in the insurance of fish farms and fish stock which saw the formation of the Aquaculture division, Aquaculture Risk (Management) Ltd, which as a wholly owned subsidiary of the Management Company, provides related technical expertise. Over the past 18 years considerable progress has been made, which now sees a world wide operation where both the Hull and Aquaculture divisions trade in some 35 countries around the world with the Membership for direct business approaching 10,000. As a specialist insurer the Company is regarded as being a world leader in the fields of fishing vessel and aquaculture risks.

The Future

Safer ships with every modern aid to navigation, stability and rescue, have not made marine insurance redundant. The centenary literature of the Royal National Mission to Deep Sea Fishermen reminds us that "ten fishermen are killed or seriously injured and three vessels lost each month". These are cruel and relentless statistics yet the Company continues to

prosper and achieve its objectives in spite of a competitive marketplace and a steady increase in the real cost of claims.

Over the period of its long history the Company has seen many changes in its specialist marketplace. The fishing industry has moved from sail through steam to diesel and is now dealing with environmental issues. The Company is a founder member of EFICA, the European Fishing Vessel Insurance Companies Association which is dedicated to the exchange of technical knowledge and mutual cooperation. The prime objective of the Company is to provide support and to respond to the changing needs of the fishing industry.

This has meant new approaches to risk control, an aspect of insurance felt to be as important as the terms and conditions of the policy of insurance itself. The Company will continue to explore new opportunities and pursue the highest standards of personal service.

Above: The Amaltal Mariner a 37m stern trawler built in Spain for a New Zealand company, which operates out of Nelson in the South Island.
Below: The Directors and Secretary of the Company pictured in 1997.

Samuel Cottam - a brush with history

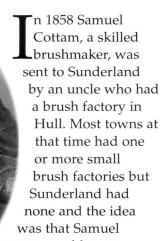

In 1858 Samuel Cottam, a skilled brushmaker, was sent to Sunderland by an uncle who had a brush factory in Hull. Most towns at that time had one or more small brush factories but Sunderland had none and the idea was that Samuel would start a new factory there funded by his uncle's business in Hull. However, before he could start, the Hull factory was totally destroyed by fire and Samuel was therefore effectively cut off.

He had however purchased a house in South Durham St., in the Hendon area of Sunderland and had tools and materials which he had brought from Hull. His home became his workshop with the basic equipment of a boring machine worked by foot, a pair of hand shears, a spoke-shave and a pitch pan for melting the hot black pitch that was used as the setting agent to retain the brush filling material in the wood head.

Above: (Top - Samuel Cottam, the founder), (bottom - George William Cottam).
Right: Hot black pitch was used as the setting agent to retain the brush filling material in the wood head. This picture dates from the 1950s.

By hard work he built up a viable business and some years later was able to move to larger premises in no. 22 Lambton Street consisting of a rather old four storied house with a large basement. On his death in 1894 his son George William Cottam took over the business and he moved with his family into the rooms above the workshop.

In 1905 the factory expanded further along into no. 23 Lambton Street and George, over a period of time was joined in the business by three of his sons Edmund, George William Jnr., and Ernest.

In 1910 Edmund as the eldest son inherited the business but there was disagreement amongst the brothers and in 1926 George William Jnr and Ernest broke away from the original company of S. Cottam & Co and started up as brushmakers in the Sheepfolds area of Monkwearmouth under the name of Cottam Brothers. The premises of this new business was a small room, part of a large stone and rubble built building which dated back to the early nineteenth century.

The first years of the new business were very difficult as this was the time of the great depression and of course the general strike but gradually the firm prospered and as it did so it expanded until by 1946 it occupied the entire building and included a wood mill so that the brush backs could be made on the premises. The factory now covered an area of approximately 10,000 square feet but the old premises were far from satisfactory.

The North East of England was an area of heavy engineering at the time e.g. shipyards, foundries and of course coal production. Additionally ports were busy with merchant ships constantly needing replenishment. The company therefore specialised in industrial and marine supplies and because of this was given help by the Government in obtaining supplies during the second world war. Production was therefore maintained during this most difficult of periods.

Goods to customers throughout the country were despatched by a mixture of road and rail transport but local deliveries were by hand cart. The cart was loaded each day and then pulled by hand across the town delivering to ironmongers, ships chandlers and various other customers. This cart was used right up until 1955 when it was replaced by a rather old Jowett van purchased for the grand sum of £87-10s.

In 1946 Cottam Brothers was incorporated as a Limited Company and the first shareholders were George William and Ernest Cottam with the latter being appointed as the company's first chairman. In 1949 George retired and was replaced by Ernest's son also named George. He was able to seek out new and more demanding customers such as the Ministry of Defence who required specialist armament brushes made to engineering standards.

Ernest retired from active participation in the Company in 1958 but remained a Director right up until his death In 1981.

As the firm took on more work the buildings became totally unsuitable for a modern factory and rather than move to new premises it was decided to rebuild on the existing site. This was commenced in September 1960 and completed in July 1962 without any break in production, although at times things got fairly desperate.

In 1963 Sunderland Corporation started to clear the residential property adjacent to the factory and it was recognised that this could provide an opportunity for further expansion.

A 99 year lease was negotiated and in the period 1967 - 70 a new production area and warehouse was built on that

Above: Making two knot brushes c1951.
Left: Stapling the material into the wood backs one tuft at a time in the early 1950s.
Top: Hand turning colliery lamp brushes in 1951.

site along with new offices on the existing site. The factory had now grown to some 22,000 square feet. Meanwhile the original family company in Lambton St., was now known as Samuel Cottam (Brushes) Ltd and had moved back to Hendon this time to Henry St. East. The company was experiencing problems and had to sell again and move to smaller premises in Norfolk St. By 1966 the firm was in financial difficulties and George Cottam, (Managing Director of Cottam Bros Ltd) acquired the company and amalgamated it into the Sheepfolds premises. In 1978 a brush manufacturer in Sheffield,

Sam'l Woodcock & Sons Ltd which dated from 1756 was for sale and Cottam Bros Ltd purchased it amalgamating it into the Sunderland operation in 1980.

During the 1980s further premises were acquired on the south side of Easington St., and then in 1994 new warehouse and office facilities were purchased in Wilson St. Nth. (the adjoining street to the factory). Excluding timber yards and other open spaces the factory and offices now cover some 40,000 square feet.

In 1976 David Cottam joined the company after having earlier qualified as a Chartered Accountant. He is the fifth generation and direct descendant of the original founder to work in the business and is now the current Managing Director and Chairman although the previous M.D. and Chairman - his father George, is still an active director of the company. The third executive director is David Irving who joined the company in 1970 and was appointed to the board as Works Director in 1987. In the early days of production, vegetable fibres, animal hair and wood were the raw materials in use. Change has not been particularly dramatic although certain animal products, e.g. whalebone, and some of the vegetable fibres are no longer available. In addition usage of many of the remaining vegetable fibres and animal hairs has declined as man-made substitutes e.g. nylon, polyester, PVC, polypropylene etc. have become available. However quite a number of the brushes still popular today would have appeared in catalogues of 100 years ago.

The really dramatic change though has been the usages to which brushes are now put. Industry has discovered many new applications and new ideas are constantly being tried. Some examples would include the oil and gas industry which uses brushes to clean and measure wear in underground and undersea pipelines; the Ministry of Defence for gun barrel cleaning; other industries would include sewage control, shotblasting, billposting, chemical spreading, cow scratcher, boot cleaners, brick manufacture, brewing etc. etc. We have long discovered that all Industry needs brushes!

Above: Roadsweeper brushes supplied to Sunderland Corporation. This picture dates from the early 1950s.
Left: A 1996 aerial view of the company's premises at Sheepfolds Industrial Estate.

Arnott Insurance - the firm with the edge

Arnott Insurance is a very well known name in Sunderland thanks to its busy office in Frederick Street, the former home of Palmers cycle shop, and for the fact that hundreds of cars carry the window sticker bearing the company slogan "We Arnott Insured."

But what is not so well known is the role the company is playing in preserving the history of the area.

For Arnott has its company headquarters at Morton House near

Fencehouses where it has created eighty jobs, and which has become one of the biggest insurance centres outside of the south east of England.

Morton House itself stands on a site where there has been a Manor for more than five hundred years. The present house was built in 1709 but the presence of gargoyles suggests they were taken from a previous house built on the same site.

The history of the Manor involves some of the best known family names in the region. The Lumleys in the fifteenth century were followed by the Belasis family in the 16th and 17th centuries who

provided Sunderland's first Mayor in Sir William Belasis. The Lambton family occupied Morton House in the l8th and 19th centuries. With such powerful families in residence it is no surprise that Morton House has played a role in the history of the land. It is known that King William I was entertained there by Sir William Belasis in 1636 which indicates that the previous building may have been a very large Tudor House.

Morton House itself was badly damaged by fire in the middle of the last century, which meant that the north and east wings had to be reconstructed. But since then little has changed. Arnott has built new offices in the walled garden but has retained all the main features of the House itself and invested in furnishings to match.

The company is proud to be playing a role in preserving local history while at the same time making a long lasting impression on the many executives from the insurance industry who visit the company.

Above: Morton House in the late 1800s.
Left: The House today complete with new wings which were added after a fire in the middle of the last century.

H. Thursby - success through enterprise

When Mr Harry Thursby came back after being demobilised from the Army in 1946, he opened up an upholsterer's shop in Wilson Street, Sunderland. Within two years he had more than a dozen men working for him and a thriving business.

The early days

For several years he toured the country, upholstering theatre and cinema seats. He confesses to having had many a 'kip' in the seats when the work was done. After a while, however, he became tired of travelling and spending prolonged periods, often three or four months, away from home.

Ironically, the last theatre he worked in was the Havelock in Sunderland, back where he started. In October 1962 he saw the reward for all his hard work when his new, spacious store opened up in Hylton Road. The new store occupied the site where his three former shops had stood.

It sold home furnishings, with all the upholstery work done by the firm's own staff at Mr Thursby's Pallion factory. He was helped in the shop by his father, also Harry, and by his 15 year old son Eric. His mother Marion kept the accounts.

Ten years later he was in the news again when he opened a new Hylton Road shop.

It stocked the American and Swedish furniture which was all the rage at the time. The extra space was used for new stock which was arranged in room settings. The old shop was to be used only for carpet sales.

A family affair

By now, Eric's brother Philip had joined the business. Eric and Philip were co-directors and responsible for buying all the furniture and carpets for the two shops. It was company policy to keep up with the latest fashions whilst giving the customer value for money and a wide choice.

To do this he visited many of the country's home furnishing exhibitions and buying well known brands of goods at a range of prices.

A discount was given for cash, 15% on furniture and 10% on carpets. Estimates and carpet fitting were free.

An attractive room setting at that time included an American table with a surface in smoked glass on a stainless steel base with four matching chairs in smoked perspex and glass fibre mixture also on steel bases. The finishing touch was added by a large optic fibre lamp which glowed in ever-changing colours and retailed at £75!

The Swedish furniture included sleek sideboards, wall units and room dividers in white lacquered wood with stainless steel handles. Also there were three piece suites designed on simple lines with comfort in mind.

Business continued to flourish and expand so that by 1995 another move became necessary.

This time business opened in Holmside in much larger premises in the city centre. By now Thursbys had a reputation for excellent customer service provable by customers having remained loyal for two and three generations.

And now
Further expansion is hoped for and planned. Carl, Eric's son, hopes to join the company when he has completed his university course. Philip's children are still very young but doubtless Thursbys will be going strong when they are old enough to stand behind the counter.

"THE COMPANY ONCE SOLD A LARGE OPTIC FIBRE LAMP WHICH GLOWED IN EVER CHANGING COLOURS AND SOLD FOR £75."

Above: Some of the 'latest' furniture on display at the store in 1972.
Facing page, bottom: The Hylton Road premises just after renovations.
Facing page, top: An advertisement dating from October 1962.

The family butchers with a traditional feel

Haswells of Silksworth is a well known family butcher in the Sunderland area. They have been butchers for almost 100 years. John Haswell, the present owner's great grandfather, was a farmer in Seaham.

He and his wife, Isabel, had six children (four daughters and two sons). They owned a very busy dairy farm for many years. The daughters encouraged their father to sell up and move from the farm into the town.

Their first butcher shop was in Seaham and in 1924 they moved to the present shop in Silksworth. At that time and for almost thirty years the shop had its own slaughter house. They made their own black pudding, sausage and dripping and prepared their own cow heels. Later they produced pies, pastries and savoury squares from a small bakery on the premises.

John Haswell's youngest son, Glanville Haswell, worked with his father on the original farm before they took over the butchers shop in Seaham. He later worked with his father at the Silksworth business and eventually, after his father's death, ran the business with his wife, Eva.

Many of the home deliveries were made by bicycle in those early days and delivery boys travelled as far as South Hyton for many years. Deliveries were made from a huge basket attached to the front of the bicycle, which the company still owns today.

"MANY OF THE EARLY HOME DELIVERIES WERE MADE ON A BICYCLE WHICH IS STILL OWNED BY THE COMPANY"

Glanville's son, John Glanville, was next in succession. He began working with his father, learning the business from his father throughout the fifties. He and his wife, Jean took over the business in 1976. They had the shop refurbished and a cold counter was put in. Deep freezing was introduced and a move was made towards serving the catering trade.

The retail business is presently being taken care of by Glanville, Jean and their two daughters, Gillian and Joanne. Mr Robert Spencer is shop manager.

The family now farms in the Durham area and supplies some of the quality beef that is sold in the shop. Haswells is a member of the Guild of Quality Butchers.

Above: Some of the vehicles used for deliveries around the North East.

Keeping Sunderland ships watertight

The remarkable history of Albert E. Taylor and Company spans almost a century and dates back to 1901 when the firm was bought by Mr. Jenneson Taylor for his son Albert Edward. The firm began at the premises at 44 Borough Road Sunderland and supplied local shipyards and engineering firms with their rubber and leather requirements, along with material to seal joints in various forms. An important early alliance was with the Scottish rubber manufacturer George Maclelland and Co.

The longest serving employee in the history of the company, Mr. W.L. Benson, retired in 1988 after completing a staggering 65 years service. He began working at Albert E. Taylor and Co. in 1918 as a 'junior delivery boy' and had risen to the position of managing director by the time he retired. Mr. Benson has vivid memories of the early days of the company and remembers Albert E. Taylor as a portly gent who always wore a blue serge suit and a button hole flower. At the time the business was supplying asbestos and rubber to local shipyards and engine works which, at the time were privately owned and operated by some well known local families such as Short's, Doxford's, Pickersgill's, Laing's and Thomson's. The company supplied items for the Thistle boats of Allen Black's, the wooden vessels constructed by Frances Fenwick and Ritson's branch boats.

When Albert E. Taylor died he was succeeded by Mr. Eric Dix, the son of a Mayor of Sunderland who also ran a successful shipping business - Friar and Dix. The business thrived in the years running up to the start of the Second World War and demand for all types of maritime rubber products soared. Rubber seals for the hatches of trawlers were a particular speciality, and when legislation was introduced requiring sea-going vessels to carry life rafts with water-tight containers for survival rations the firm was quick to exploit the potential. When Eric Dix, who was a captain in the Army, was called up for war service he successfully requested that W. L. Benson be exempted from the call up in order that he could take control of the company and ensure that it continued to produce the essential supplies for the war effort. Many vessels were being converted to Naval use - such as mine sweepers and sealing rubbers for hatches and doors were needed from reliable, efficient suppliers. Orders such as one for waterproof coats for the Nation's A.R.P Wardens soon followed and the firm prospered. In 1961 Mr. Dix changed the status of the firm to a limited liability company under the title of A. E. Taylor (Sunderland) Ltd., with a capital of £9802 - the odd £2 in this sum belonging to W.L. Benson. Sadly Mr. Dix passed away in 1968 and his sister, whose husband was the owner of the Yorkshire Relish Company appointed Mr. W. L. Benson managing director in January 1969. The firm enjoyed a further period of increasing prosperity under Mr Benson until he retired in 1983. Two former colleagues, Mr. Brian Barrass, nephew of W. L. Benson and Mr. Bryan Temple then took up the reins and have now both worked for the company for more than 35 years.

During the period between 1938 and 1988 every vessel constructed in the shipyards of Sunderland used hoses, rubber joints and other fittings supplied by the Albert E. Taylor and Company - a remarkable achievement for such a small company.

The decline of the ship building and engineering industries caused a shift in the manufacturing activities pursued by the company. The firm now concentrates on the conversion of polythene into bags, sheets and covers for numerous uses.

Above: A page from an early catalogue showing just a small example of the many rubber products that A. E. Taylor produced at the time.
Left: The firm's premises on Borough Road, Sunderland.

A flat in Wear Garth, thoughtfully decorated for the Queen's Coronation in 1953

ACKNOWLEDGMENTS

THE PUBLISHERS WOULD LIKE TO THANK THE FOLLOWING ORGANISATIONS
FOR THEIR HELP IN THE PRODUCTION OF THIS BOOK

BEAMISH PHOTOGRAPH LIBRARY AT BEAMISH MUSEUM

NEWCASTLE CHRONICLE & JOURNAL LIMITED

SUNDERLAND MUSEUM AND ART GALLERY